KIDS AND MONEY

Teaching Financial Responsibility
and Values to Children

Other Titles by Connie Ragen Green

Living the Mentored Life

Rethinking the Work Ethic: Embrace the Struggle and Exceed Your Own Potential

Doing What It Takes: The Online Entrepreneur's Playbook Book. Blog. Broadcast. – The Trifecta of Entrepreneurial Success

Write Publish Prosper: How to Write Prolifically, Publish Globally, and Prosper Eternally

The Transformational Entrepreneur: Creating a Life of Dedication and Service

Living the Internet Lifestyle: Quit Your Job, Become an Entrepreneur, and Live Your Ideal Life

The Inner Game of Internet Marketing

The Weekend Marketer: Say Goodbye to the "9 to 5", Build an Online Business, and Live the Life You Love

What is Your Why?

Time Management Strategies for Entrepreneurs: How to Manage Your Time to Increase Your Bottom Line

Huge Profits with Affiliate Marketing: How to Build an Online Empire by Recommending What You Love

Membership Sites Made Simple

Article Marketing: How to Attract New Prospects, Create Products, and Increase Your Income

Targeted Traffic Techniques

Huge Profits with a Tiny List: 50 Ways to Use Relationship Marketing to Increase Your Bottom Line

KIDS AND MONEY

Teaching Financial Responsibility and Values to Children

By Connie Ragen Green

Copyright © 2018 by Hunter's Moon Publishing

ISBN Paperback: 978-1-937988-39-5
ISBN Kindle: 978-1-937988-40-1

Hunter's Moon Publishing
http://HuntersMoonPublishing.com

Dedication

To Kathy McClendon, a friend and so much more for over thirty years, so far. We met in a real estate class at the community college and you helped me to become a certified residential appraiser the following year. I was struck by your kindness and generosity in a world where neither is common or expected and both are greatly appreciated and knew right then you were a very special human being.

Thank you for playing so many roles in my life throughout the decades. These include, but are not limited to: big sister, financial advisor, fashion consultant, and good listener. You share without holding back, teach without lecturing, and listen without judging.

You may not know that I was picking up tips from you and evolving with my own beliefs and values around money and investing as I observed the brilliant way you handled so many aspects of your life over the years. And no matter where I was or what I was doing during this time I knew that you were always just a phone call away.

Thank you for being there for me and please know that much of what I've included in this book is based on what I have learned, implemented, and internalized from knowing you. I could not have asked for a better role model during my lifetime and know that God sent you to me as a special gift.

Table of Contents

Other Titles by Connie Ragen Green.................................ii

Dedication.. v

Foreword 1

Preface 4

Introduction... 6

What Is Financial Responsibility?................................... 9

The History of Money 12

Financial Beliefs and Values..19

Using Money in Today's World.......................................26

Why is Financial Responsibility Important? 34

Raising Financially Responsible Children 36

Your Child's "Money Personality".................................44

Entrepreneurship versus Working for Others 52

What If We Teach Financial Responsibility?...................62

The Financially Aware Adult 66

A Limitless Future..73

How Do You Teach Financial Responsibility?.................80

Allowances and Earning Income....................................83

Saving, Spending, Investing, and Giving.........................93

What's Next?.. 104

It's a Family Affair 105

Beliefs and Practices at Every Stage of Life 117

Conclusion 128

Appendix: Budgeting With Children............................. 130

About the Author.. 149

Foreword

It was my pleasure and good fortune to meet Connie back in 1984. This was not too long after she had taken her exam to become a licensed real estate agent. She was anxious to learn as much as she could on this topic and to be of great service to her clients. When she knocked on our door one Saturday morning as a part of her "farming" efforts to meet more homeowners in our area my wife and I knew we had found the person we wanted to have represent us to sell our home that summer.

It wasn't because she had the experience; she had been licensed for less than two years at that time. And it wasn't because she knew the ins and outs of real estate transactions, financing, or marketing a home like ours (a Craftsman home built by Greene and Greene in 1917); she had previously only listed and sold tract homes and modern custom built homes as a part of her daily work.

We insisted on working with Connie because of her honest and straightforward manner, and her willingness to find the answers to the questions she encountered that she did not have ready and accurate answers to when we, or anyone else for that matter, asked.

She not only listed and sold our home in record time; she also found us an excellent guest house in the area we leased while we were deciding whether to build a new home or to relocate to the East Coast. As it turned out, it was one of the smartest decisions we made that year to stay put in southern California, and part of that was based on what transpired a few months later.

Without going into too much detail about real estate, I will tell you that at that time banking institutions were going through some major changes in the United States, and that was causing a domino effect around the world. A large part of this was based on a common legal practice at that time, known as a wraparound mortgage, or a "wrap", and something that eventually evolved into something officially referred to as an REIT (real estate investment trust) agreement.

To make a long and fascinating story a little shorter, there was a window of time where anyone could assume a loan on a property without having to qualify and without the fear of the lender "calling" the loan due and payable when it transferred title. This was an excellent opportunity, especially for a person who had little or no money for a down payment, a less than stellar credit score, and insufficient income to qualify for a conventional loan. That described most of the population, yet few were aware of this situation and therefore not able to act on it. We certainly did not know about it, and we considered ourselves to be savvy investors.

When Connie first got wind of this situation she sprang into action and became a real estate mogul, at least in our little corner of the world. She came to my wife and me with some information and details, and we came aboard, along with a dozen or so others who wanted to invest in an area north of Los Angeles known as the San Fernando Valley.

Before the window closed, we had all purchased single family, duplex, and triplex properties using this system. And Connie went above and beyond to ensure that we were all given the proper legal and tax advice for our specific situations by her own team of experts she had quickly but astutely assembled so there would be no unpleasant surprises in the future.

She not only earned the commission on these purchases, but had also picked up six single family investment homes of her own. One was on a busy street and needed much work. I can still recall her sharing the details of how she readied it to be a rental, including seeding the front lawn herself and bringing along a trusted friend to water and tend to it as the new blades of grass finally appeared, and also purchasing and installing carpet remnants that would make this house a home for the new tenants.

Several years later Connie put together an LLC for a group of us to purchase an apartment building, something none of us would have been able to do on our own. That's a story for another time, but suffice it to say that Connie Green is someone you want to know if you are interested in real estate investing of any kind.

I wish her only the best success with this book and cannot recommend her highly enough as someone to turn to for advice on a variety of topics around finance. And my wife, Allison wanted me to add that everything Connie gets involved in she does from her heart, so you are in good hands when you choose to work with her or to become a friend, both of which we have done over these past three decades.

Marshall Hale
Toluca Lake, California

Preface

The idea for this book came forth as I was having a discussion about money in general and beliefs and values more specifically with members of the Mastermind I am a part of in Santa Barbara. As we sat around our table at the Santa Barbara Club, sharing breakfast prepared by our private chef and meaningful stories on topics of great interest and medium importance on a sunny Friday morning, I realized that the way I am living right now is a direct result of the lessons, values, and beliefs around money I learned from a variety of people while I was growing up. Because almost all of the people in my Mastermind had a very different background and upbringing than I did growing up, at first I thought they would not understand money values and financial responsibility from my perspective.

That turned out to be a misconception on my part. Each of these people is self-made in their own way as a result of the specific actions, some well thought out and others purely by accident they took and continue to take each day throughout their lives. And as for me, by taking the time and making the effort to expand upon what was instilled in me from a young age I have been able to create a life for myself that most people only dream of and most will never bring to fruition.

The ideas and concepts we discussed that morning got the wheels turning in my mind. What if I could share my thoughts and ideas on this topic to readers everywhere, enabling them to have more of an influence on the children in their lives? The possibilities are endless, and this all stems from being aware that what we say and do impacts kids in a far different way than it does with adults. I began to scribble some notes while I was still sitting at the table and began outlining a book soon after. My Mastermind partners are used to that behavior from me and often joke that when I get that faraway look in my eyes and take out my notepad a new book is soon to follow.

If only parents, grandparents, teachers, and other adult role models had tools at their disposal and a plan in their minds and hearts to consciously teach financial responsibility and values around money to the children in their life. What if every child had at least one adult who would take the time to discuss the details of what money is and how it can make a difference in life, if understood on a level that few achieve even well into adulthood?

Growing up as a child of poverty and reaching the financial goals I have attained as an adult has made me realize and understand so much that I want others to know while they are still in their formative years. Money is not about the material things it can buy and the lifestyles that have no substance. Wealth is a state of mind that is achievable by anyone who learns about the importance of values, beliefs, and traditions around money that will be passed on for generations to come.

It is my hope that my simplified explanations, stories, and exercises included in this book will guide you to thinking a little differently about this important subject, starting the conversation in a way that can become a natural dialogue, and that it will lead to meaningful discussions and interactions between you and the child in your life. Passing on this type of wisdom can have far reaching effects, and may even help ensure that our planet moves forward in a smarter and more empathetic way for future generations.

May you enjoy your life journey as much as I am enjoying sharing this information with you.

Introduction

You can expect to read about many of my own experiences when it comes to beliefs and values around money within these pages. The first section asks the question "What is financial responsibility?" We must compare and contrast this question in order to be better prepared to approach the subject within our family and with the child or children in our lives.

I begin with a historical discussion and explanation of what money is, where it began originally, and how we went from a system of simple barter to one of more complex trading, and moved on to coins and paper money. Then we move into a discussion of your earliest memories and experiences with money to give yourself a jumping off point into what financial responsibility truly is and what it means to you. After that we discuss how our concept of money has evolved during our lifetime as a way to dig more deeply into how this has shaped our life experiences.

Next, we think about the financial beliefs and values we currently hold, how this all began to take shape when we were very young children, and thinking back to the early experiences and memories of how and where we began earning money of our own. These early beliefs can be changed, or at least altered as we grow older and will lead to how we value and use our money now, the difference between needs and wants, and the ideas around giving, tithing, and donating money to individuals and group. Changing your beliefs around money and the "needs versus wants" question is also included in this section.

In the second section on why financial responsibility and values are important we explore how to determine your child's financial "personality" and whether your child is more suited for the life of a small business owner, that of an entrepreneur, or as an employee. Nurturing your child's beliefs and values is a crucial piece around this topic.

What if you teach financial responsibility to your children? is the question that leads off the third section, and here we explore the often overlooked concept of living within your means and seeing the payoff from having self-control and discipline in the area of money and finances. Being prepared for those inevitable rainy days allows for a limitless future.

The fourth section is where we get into the meat of this topic and I share how you can begin to teach financial responsibility and values to the child or children in your life. I am known to be contrarian and controversial on the subject of allowances for children and fully expect you to disagree vehemently with me on much of what I have to say.

Remember this writing is intended to serve as an open and honest discussion, with no right or wrong answers even possible. From differing opinions comes true growth and change, so instead of embracing my thoughts and ideas I would prefer for you to come up with your own set of rules, customs, and traditions, as well as a foundation on which to build within your own family for the benefit of your children. Also included in this section are some ideas around the earning, saving, spending, investing, and giving of money for the child in your life.

Finally, in the section on What's Next? we will discuss beliefs and practices at every stage of life, generational values through the ages, and the importance of addressing and dealing with financial stress in children. This is a growing issue in our society that has far reaching implications.

I've added an Appendix on "Budgeting with Children" that I hope will be of value to your entire family. My experience has shown me that even though having enough money is optimal, being forced to watch every penny is an educational experience that can be turned into fun for children. Perhaps we come to be grateful for and appreciate money all the more when it doesn't come so easily.

I expect your thoughts and takeaways after reading this book and going through the exercises to be ones that are based on your own beliefs and values and the conclusions you come to at the end of each chapter and section. No size will ever fit all when it comes to the topic of financial responsibility and values around money, so finding your own path and taking the journey alongside your children is bound to be one you will not want to miss.

What Is Financial Responsibility?

Making money is art and working is
art and good business is the best art.
~ Andy Warhol

We've all known someone who was irresponsible when it came to handling money. As a child, I had friends whose allowance was spent or at least spoken for long before they received it and for whom money was simply something to shuffle off without thinking. Teenagers can sometimes burn through money faster than what seems humanly possible as it burns a hole in their pocket. Young adults may find themselves short at the beginning of the month for their rent money or their car payment and may even be using credit cards to purchase food items.

These are all examples of what can happen if financial responsibility is not taught at an early age and in a way that makes an indelible print on the mind of the person receiving the knowledge and information from someone they know and respect. We simply cannot expect the children in our lives to become financially prudent adults without the guidance and nurturing based on our experiences and results. This would be tantamount to expecting someone to understand science or geography without the foundation and ongoing education necessary to and involved in these areas. No one can conduct a science experiment or read a map unless they have been instructed on how to do so. Likewise, we cannot expect a young person to automatically understand how to earn, save, spend, and give unless they have been guided every step of the way.

Spending money without first thinking, earning money in a way that does not suit your personality, failing to save or invest money regularly, and not respecting and valuing money can lead to unnecessary hardship along life's journey. Add to that an unwillingness to give to those in need and you have a human being who may lack empathy and have issues with some of their interpersonal relationships throughout their lifetime. This need not be the case if you teach these concepts along the way using real life examples and additional training.

Even if the schools your child attends choose to touch on this subject matter, and most do not, it may not be close to being a complete financial training and will not reflect the values and beliefs you hold dear within your family. Financial education must be a personal and ongoing commitment to ensure that the child in your life has the opportunity to live a life that is rewarding and fulfilling as a result of sound financial decisions made each and every day, with every dollar that is earned, saved, invested, and spent.

The difficulty may come when you, as the responsible adult in the relationship, realize that you did not have the proper training as you were growing up and lack some basic knowledge in this area. Is it too late to make up the deficit in your own financial education in order to help the child or children in your life now? No! It is never too late, and in fact it may be even more beneficial to learn about money right along with your child. Being able to look yourself in the mirror and honestly know that you are knowledgeable about finances is a gift you must give to yourself and then share with those around you, including the youngest members of your family.

The joy and satisfaction of becoming a financially responsible adult will carry you through the remainder of your life with a distinct advantage, and allow you to pass this knowledge and experience on to generations to come. This is a legacy that will be meaningful to many and will make their lives easier and more fulfilled.

Knowing that you are living within or even below your means gives you the chance to have peace of mind in your day to day life. You will always be prepared for an upcoming "rainy day" and may even be able to take advantage of opportunities that present themselves when it comes to relocating, changing jobs, or adjusting to a change in circumstances in your personal life.

Imagine a world where you are in charge and call the shots, rather than having to pass up something because you lack the funds to follow through. And as you go through your life there will be others in your family who are affected as well by your level of responsibility when it comes to your finances. A child may want to attend a music camp or a spouse may want to return to school for advanced education in a specialty area. Having control of your finances means that every decision is based on the results that are possible and not limited by money.

Let's discuss what financial responsibility is so that we can lay a foundation for approaching this topic in a way that makes sense to you and your family and will also get you thinking about this and then starting the conversation with the kids in your life.

The History of Money

As I began thinking about and subsequently researching my ideas for this book, I began to think about the history of money. I knew that bartering was an early method of paying for what you wanted and needed, and that gold and silver represented early forms of currency, but I knew it would be important to share more details about how money came to be before I could continue with a discussion of how to teach the child or children in your life about valuing and respecting money. We must understand what something is and its origins if we expect others to form their own values and beliefs. I believe this is the very best way when seeking positive outcomes as kids grow into financially responsible adults.

Where Did Money Come From?

Bartering was the original method of exchanging something you had an excess of, such as cattle or grain, for something that you needed, perhaps salt or tools. It's an excellent idea, if you stop to think about it. Two people come face to face and agree to trade items back and forth in a way where each side benefits. If it feels like a fair exchange, it's a done deal. I have bartered in my business many times, like during my first year working as an online entrepreneur when I bartered for the technical skills of someone who was seeking help with marketing. This arrangement lasted for two years, at which time I began to pay for her services. Most recently I bartered for editing from someone who needed help with writing and marketing. As a child you may have bartered by trading baseball cards or other collectibles. This is the most basic form of exchange that has gone on since the beginning of time.

Coins and Currency

As we became more global in our interactions sometime around 1,100 B.C., exchanging livestock and other items became less attractive and the result was coins made of bronze, silver, and gold that represented the value of these metals. This began in China and the first minted coins were made around 600 B.C. in Lydia, which is now known as the western coast of Turkey. But carrying bags of coins was cumbersome and not the safest of practices, so by the 7th Century A.D. paper currency came into existence, first in China and then in Sweden and other parts of Europe. This was a great help - boon - to international trade as traders and others were then able to purchase goods from faraway lands using the currency of their country.

This created a market for currency and this led to money becoming a political situation for the first time in recorded history. If your country had a stable government or monarchy, then you had a better opportunity to become a part of the international trading market. Currency wars erupted from time to time and currency from one country was at least temporarily devalued. This caused prices to fluctuate over time and sometimes led to price gouging and elimination of currency from the international marketplace.

I'd also like to point out here that most people in the world were illiterate until the nineteenth century, and that money in all forms needed to be designed in order for the masses to understand and be treated fairly when it came to financial transactions.

Credit became available in Europe in Medieval times with the creation of something they called "tally sticks." Notches were made on a wooden stick to show exactly how much someone owed or had lent. The merchants then cut the tally stick down the middle so that both the borrower and the lender had a record of the amounts. This method was also used in England for hundreds of years as a way to collect and record taxes from citizens in each village. At some point counterfeiting became an issue, and it was almost impossible for anyone to make a replica of the wooden tally stick.

Counterfeiting was punishable by death in many parts of the world, and is still a federal offense in the United States. I was in banking during my early twenties and had experience with this on a few different levels. I will never forget the man who came in to the bank to make his mortgage payment with twelve hundred dollar bills. The teller's routine inspection of this currency showed them all to be counterfeit and they were seized from the customer. The FBI was called in and the man was asked to share where he had obtained this money. When he was reluctant to answer he was arrested and taken away in handcuffs. That was a sobering moment for everyone there that day, as none of us had ever considered the consequences of being in possession of counterfeit currency.

From the mid 1800s until 1971, the United States and much of the world was on something referred to as the "Gold Standard." This meant that our currency was backed by something of real value - the gold. The United States held most of the world's gold supply, but this system had many downfalls over the years.

I believe that the history of money is a topic worthy of further study and exploration when it comes to learning about financial responsibility. At least in my experience in the school system, this is not an area that is taught in any great detail. I have oversimplified the concepts I am touching upon here and would encourage you to make the time to discuss this with the child or children in your life as a way to bring these ideas to life and to top of mind thinking.

Early Experiences and Memories Around Money

I believe the first memories I had about money came when I was getting ready to start first grade. We had moved and somehow my good shoes had gotten lost in the shuffle. My mother took me to buy new shoes and we came home with six pairs that day. It was a day I would never forget, because although the shoes had been on sale I still felt like the richest person in the world when it came to material possessions. I can remember sitting on the floor in the living room of our small apartment and trying on each shoe very carefully, and then walking back and forth to see and feel and experience what it was like to own so many pairs of new shoes. I mixed and matched the shoes I tried on, thoroughly enjoying this experience and the sensation it evoked. Some of them were made of leather and I can even remember the deep breaths I took to smell what new shoes were like.

That feeling was short-lived, for it wasn't long before the reality of my situation settled in. We were poor. Not just poor, but living below the poverty level. Before the end of the first grade I would know what it was like to go to bed and then wake up hungry, to be teased by children at school because my clothes were too well worn, and to come home one day to find a paper taped to the front door by the local sheriff telling us we had just three days to pay up or move out.

It was just my mother and I, and for reasons unknown to me until adulthood my father never contributed financially after he and my mother divorced when I was three years old. My mother did her best at the time, but she had some health issues that kept her from working full time. Also, she had come from a time where a mother was home with her children so she was always there to take me to school and to pick me up afterwards for the walk home.

We never had a car or a telephone or even a permanent place to live while I was in elementary school. Twice before I finished the sixth grade we were homeless, and each of those times people took us in until we found a new place to live. Of course, no one at school knew any of this and I became adept at disguising and masking our situation in order to save face and fit in with the other kids. Looking back, I guess I lied about many things and did not understand at the time why this was so wrong. It was the beginning of self-preservation, in my eyes.

My mother was an artist, and also took some office jobs at times. Whenever she would earn some money we would take the bus downtown to celebrate, even if it was a school day. She would buy makeup and some other personal things for herself, and then buy me clothes and shoes and something else just for fun. And even though my memories of these shopping trips downtown are good ones, if I peel back a layer they become very sad times in my mind. We were in an endless loop of poverty, having a little money to spend, and then back to poverty and never having enough right then or for a rainy day.

We had few relatives, and my father seldom came around for a visit. But we did have some friends and neighbors who would help from time to time. I can remember receiving a gorgeous leather wallet from one neighbor on my birthday, and inside was a crisp five dollar bill. He explained to my mother and I that it was good luck to include some money when you gave someone a wallet or a purse as a gift, and it was with this interaction I began to associate having enough money to pay for the things we needed with being lucky.

So many messages and images and experiences were all thrown together in my head and soon I was more confused than ever about money and what it represented to me. This all changed when I began earning some money of my own, and I share some of these experiences with you in the next chapter.

It's both funny and interesting how a simple act, like giving or receiving a gift, choosing between one item and another, and deciding to do some work in return for money sets the stage for your relationship with money from the time you are a young child. In my case, everything that occurred and was a part of my life experience as a child was purely accidental and coincidental.

What you choose for the child in your life can be more planned and intentional. This can become even more complex if you choose it to be, so I am suggesting that you take into account the personality of the child you will be influencing and teaching about finances and financial responsibility, along with values and beliefs around money that will last a lifetime.

Even though your story and your experiences have shaped your own beliefs and values, limit how much of that you pass on to children. You want them to learn from a combination of their own experiences, and the examples you set forth both overtly and covertly. Something you say in passing or do without much thought can become imprinted on the mind of someone much younger than yourself.

How Has the Concept of Money Evolved During Your Lifetime?

It's likely that what you say, do, and believe about money at this stage of your life has changed significantly since you came of age. If we are all the culmination of our thoughts and experiences, then it makes sense that we can purposely change our thinking, learn and grow, and become a changed person in almost any area of our life where we choose to do so. If this is indeed the way life works, then we are free to do a reset on our beliefs and values around finances, as well as our subsequent actions.

Think about the person you were when you finished high school or had entered college. Do this as a written activity if you choose.

Ask yourself these questions and see what comes up for you:

- Did you have a job while you were still in high school?
- Was this by choice, or was it necessary in order to pay for a car or other expenses?
- How did the conversation come up at home or with a counselor at your high school about how you would pay for your college education?
- While you were in college, how did you perceive financial responsibility?
- Once you were ready to begin your career, was money a determining factor in your choice of job?
- While you were in your twenties were you totally independent of others financially?
- When did you begin to save and invest as an adult?

The answers to these questions are your history of money, the topic of this chapter, but in a manner that is personalized to you. And as with all historical information, it changes with every thought and idea that is put into action. Think about how you want your history to unfold, and how you can be a part of the history for the child or children in your life when it comes to money and financial responsibility. If you want this history to have a different outcome and place in the history books, it may be time to take action and start the rewriting process in your own life.

Financial Beliefs
and Values

What I Learned as a Child

It is my belief that we learn about all aspects of money from an early age from our parents and others around us. This can begin as early as four or five years old and will shape our thoughts, beliefs, values, and experiences as we grow older. If we wish to change our relationship with money, we must make a conscious choice to do so and become active in our quest to create a new belief system for the remainder of our lives.

I was raised primarily by a single mother who had grown up during the Great Depression. From the time I was a very little girl I heard stories about how hard it was for her family during this time. Her father, my grandfather was able to keep his job during those difficult years because he was a salesman for a company that sold equipment to fire departments across the United States. But this meant that we would be away from home for weeks on end and not know how much he had earned until the orders came in.

My grandmother did laundry and ironing for a wealthy family in their rural town in Missouri, and my two uncles worked part-time at the local grocery store, bagging groceries and stocking shelves in return for bags of potatoes and day old bread at the end of their shift each day. My mother was the youngest, and finally she was able to get a job at a local factory after school. Her parents insisted she stay in school, but working the night shift didn't allow her enough time to study properly.

What my mother passed on to me was the fear that comes from not having enough money to pay for the basic necessities of life. Growing up we didn't have a car or a telephone. When I was in the fourth grade another girl in my class at school asked me for my phone number. I gave her and the other girls the number of a pay phone one block from my house. Most afternoons after school I could be found sitting on the sidewalk in front of that payphone, reading and finishing up any homework and waiting for the phone to ring. No one ever found out about that and the lesson I learned was one of doing what was necessary to fit in.

By the time I was eleven years old I was babysitting, mowing lawns, and doing all types of odd jobs in my neighborhood to help bring in some much needed money to our household.

I learned to equate hard work with financial stability, and my mother also taught me that education was the only way out of poverty. By the time I was in college I lived in fear of not having enough money to pay the rent, buy food, and maintain a vehicle. I often felt guilty when I purchased new clothing, school supplies, or other items for myself.

Working as a waitress from the time I was a young teenager gave me spending money on a regular basis, and at some point I became extremely generous with my friends who did not have part-time jobs while they were in school. I can remember one Saturday taking the bus to the local shopping area with two of my girlfriends and buying them each a new blouse and a pair of pants. This felt so good and they were very appreciative, but I believe this action set up a belief system in my mind that people would like me more if I bought them things. I also began to believe that my worth was tied to how much money I had. I saved half of what I was earning during those years and spent the other half on frivolous items for myself and others.

As a young adult I became more of a risk taker with money, spending on things that I believed would earn me a higher than average ROI (return on investment). By the time I was in my early twenties I was buying run down houses to fix up and resell and eventually got my real estate license to have access to the better deals.

By that time I had stopped saving money on my own, and instead kept telling myself that I could earn more money to make up for anything I lost in a real estate investment. This strategy is a poor one without a safety net or a future. And back then I did not have anyone to teach me about money or investments so I was on a trapeze without a net.

I maintained my belief that working hard was the path to wealth, and when I became a classroom teacher at age thirty I knew I would not give up my real estate license. If anything, I increased my work as a broker and finally a residential appraiser after becoming a teacher because we went on strike the first year and the fear of not having enough money to pay my bills hit me hard and reminded me of stories my mother had told me as a child.

My Early Work Experiences

The very first time I remember earning money as a child came during the summer I turned eleven years old. One of my friends had three young cousins and her aunt, their mother needed to spend the evening doing a variety of errands that were not suitable with three little boys in tow. She knocked on our door around six-thirty on a Friday night, quickly asked my mother if I could babysit for a couple of hours that evening, and when my mother got the nod of approval from me the deal was done. They lived right across the street from us and I knew my mother would keep the living room curtains open and check on me every fifteen minutes or so.

I spent about four hours with the boys, all under five years old, and managed to entertain them, feed them, and change diapers without too much of a fuss. Then I read them stories until they fell asleep on their sofa around ten o'clock that night.

When their mother returned she was kind and appreciative and thanked me as she squeezed two wadded up five dollar bills into my hand. I'm sure I said thank you before heading home, but the truth was that I had not anticipated being paid for watching her children. Looking back, this was a turning point in my life and my thinking, where I finally understood that I had value to others that could earn me some money in the coming years.

I showed my mother the money and she told me I could go to the mall the following afternoon to spend it. There was no discussion around saving even part of the ten dollars I had earned, or about what I might buy at the shopping center. The message I received was one of "easy come, easy go" when it came to suddenly having money that was not planned. But somewhere in the recesses of my mind I had a different plan, and it was to save half and to spend half on something meaningful. I did just that, and the purchase I made was for a pair of white, satin leather pumps for my mother. I told her it was a late Mother's Day gift and she wore them proudly until they finally fell apart a few years later.

After that I sought out opportunities to earn money, and they seemed to magically appear on a regular basis. I became partners with the boy next door and we started a lawn mowing business that summer. He and I also did some amateur landscaping, based on his talent and experience helping his father and older brother with their yard, and we also raised gerbils to sell to the local pet stores.

Another business endeavor that began that summer was a babysitting service with five of my girlfriends. We worked in teams of two girls each and offered child care services for single mothers who had taken summer jobs and didn't have anyone to watch their children while they were working all day long. Remember this was the late 1960s, when the rules, laws, and common practices of the American public were much looser than they would become in the near future.

This babysitting business was a more serious undertaking that I had anticipated and we had to halt our services midway through the summer because of the situations that arose. It was a learning experience in that I would now give more thought to the services I would offer and the clients I would take.

When school began I put my entrepreneurship on hold and didn't give it another thought until the following spring and summer. Then I was back at it with new dreams, goals, and ideas on how to earn money for back to school clothes, supplies, and a new bicycle, as well as helping my mother with our household expenses. And because I had stuck to my gut feeling about the importance of saving half of every penny I earned, the year in between had been a prosperous one for my mother and I. Whenever we were short of money I would pull out five dollars from my secret dresser drawer and we would have enough for our needs.

The first time I was an official employee was when a family moved in across the street from us and we learned that the father would be the new manager of the Uncle John's Pancake House a few blocks from us. I'll share more about this adventure in the coming chapters, and about how this one job shaped my financial future for the next three decades, for sure.

How I Changed My Beliefs Around Money

Having grown up in poverty, it made sense that I would come of age having a variety of issues around money. My solution was to become a student of finance, and this began

23

while I was at UCLA. Even though finance and economics was not the field I was majoring in or planning to work in once I graduated, I took as many courses as possible in these areas as my chosen electives.

Upon graduation I began an informal study of real estate and became first a licensed real estate agent and a few years later a broker. Several years after that I became a Certified Residential Appraiser to expand upon my knowledge. And I didn't simply study for and earn these licenses; I worked in real estate full time for about five years and then on a part-time basis during the twenty years I was working as a classroom teacher.

And even though my training and education may have seemed to be slow progress from the perspective of those around me, it was at the perfect pace for me at the time. With every transaction and situation I learned valuable lessons that allowed/permitted me to delve deeper into a world that had previously eluded me.

When I think back to my first real estate transaction at age twelve when I purchased the raw land parcel, to the first home I purchased before age twenty-one, I view these as my training ground for what was to come. Each transaction was meaningful to me in multiple ways as I learned and internalized concepts that would forge the beliefs and values around money I would hold and expand upon as a financially responsible adult.

These days I consider myself to be someone who can be frugal and downright cheap at times, especially when it comes to purchasing things for myself, but knowledgeable and generous at other times when making purchases for the people I care most about in my life.

Our mindset is a combination of our choices and experiences, so I will recommend that you begin giving greater thought to both as you go through life and have an impact on the children around you. Being instrumental in the financial education and choices of a young person can be simultaneously frustrating and rewarding, and it is only by these experiences that the child or children in your life can grow into financially responsible adults.

It is said that good morals and ethics are based on the words and actions we choose when no one is looking, and if this is indeed the case then it is also determined by the choices we make with money when we are alone. Ordering the hamburger without fries in order to purchase a drink or dessert may seem like a spur of the moment decision, but it is actually the culmination of our thoughts, beliefs, and values around money. Let's move on now to one of the most important topics you will encounter, that of being able to adequately distinguish between items you truly need and those you simple want to have in your life.

Using Money in Today's World

Needs Versus Wants - Deciding What to Buy

The majority of people living on the planet right now have little or no disposable income. On a daily basis they are more concerned with having clean water to drink, enough food to eat, a clean place to sleep, and a safe environment in which to raise their family. I'm involved with an international service organization called Rotary, so this information is top of mind for me, along with helping wherever I can. One of the goals of Rotary is to eradicate polio from our planet, and over the past thirty years we have made great strides by focusing on the countries in which this disease is prevalent.

The people you and I know most likely give little thought to any of what I have just mentioned with any regularity, even though I believe that everyone does care about people in general. Instead, they are concerned with raising their standard of living in ways that are more common in the first world countries where we live. This all boils down to understanding "needs" versus "wants", two concepts that become muddied over time when we are not exposed to them as a part of learning financial responsibility.

We all *need* clean drinking water in order to survive. We *want* water that tastes good.

This is a simplistic example of the difference between wants and needs, but one that can be used as the standard against everything else we choose or desire in our daily lives. Breaking it down this way for the child or children in your life will help them to step back and appreciate all of the material things they already have, and about how we can all get along with much less than we have.

Three years ago I decided to stop buying so much stuff. I live in two cities and have homes in each. When I took inventory in the five bathrooms I have in total I was shocked at what I found. Evidently I am, or was a collector of shampoo, bar soap, and hand lotion. I am embarrassed to tell you how much of this I owned at that time, but suffice it to say I could have opened a small boutique with the inventory I had on hand. And most of it was excellent quality and made by companies you may recognize.

The sad part was that I could not even remember when and where I had purchased most of these items. Some were still in their original packaging and some was still in the bags along with the receipts showing when I had made the purchase and the amount I had paid. I was ashamed of myself on that day and decided to stop the madness right then and there.

I still have not purchased shampoo since that day three years ago, but I will most likely run out before this year is through. I have also gifted much of the soaps and lotions to others, including friends, family members, and to charitable groups I am a part of that distribute those items to people in need. That has been a joyous process for me and one I will continue for the remainder of my life. And I have learned my lesson with over buying once and for all.

Let's get back to the discussion of needs versus wants. For me, this concept is now clearer than ever and one I have embraced each day.

I just completed a one year moratorium on buying any type of clothing item or shoes. Once again, I had discovered that my huge closets were bursting at the seams, and during my year I figured out that I had saved, or not spent about three thousand dollars. And I still have items that have their original tags on them. It's fun these days for me to go shopping in my own closet. I have also given away twice as many clothing items and shoes as I was used to giving to others in the past.

In my case, this is an example of conspicuous consumption, a phenomenon that is all too common in first world countries among the middle classes and the affluent. Financial responsibility includes consuming only the amount we need and sharing what we own and do not need with people who are in need.

I challenge you to look around and take inventory of what you own right now. Giving away the excess and slowing down your purchasing will be a weight off your shoulders, literally. And giving thought to each and every item to see if it is honestly something that we need or something we simply want will put you on the path of greater financial responsibility than almost any other single action.

There is a good reason that public storage units are one of the fastest growing businesses and one of the best investments.

To Save or To Spend?

When children are given money, their first response is to want to spend it. Typically, this purchase will be for something they have been wanting but have been denied by their parents, the people holding the purse strings. But often they could have the first reaction to having some money of their own to purchase something for someone else, perhaps as a gift for a birthday or other special occasion. Seldom is the first response from a child with newfound money "I can't wait to save this!"

Saving is not a natural thought or idea unless it has been taught, discussed, and modeled by adults in the child's life, or older children in the family. To deny yourself something you want and now have the money in hand with which to purchase this item is a foreign idea to all of us when we are young. But once the concept of saving is taught and explained, everything changes forever.

I was ten years old when I had my first savings account at our local bank. It was at my mother's suggestion and we opened up the account with three dollars I had saved up from nickel and diming her over the past month. I will never forget the feeling of pride I experienced as the teller handed me the little book that represented my savings account. The amount was written in ink, and next to it were the date stamp and the teller's initials. That book became one of my most prized possessions that year, and my goal was to add to the balance as often as possible. It was from this first bank account that I learned the concept of saving towards a specific goal. First it was for a bicycle, and when I withdrew the sixty dollars and walked over to the Schwinn store to purchase my blue stingray with a white banana seat and high handlebars I was quite proud of myself. This had left a balance of only five dollars in my savings account that day, and as I rode home that day I was thinking of how to add more to my account as soon as possible. I was riding high in the saddle, or at least in my banana seat and thought the world to be a place of opportunity and adventure.

During next few years, leading into my teenage years I was constantly torn between spending and saving. For as much as I wanted to buy things, I also experienced great joy when my balance increased. My tiny account book was dog-eared by now, and when I filled up all the pages the bank's manager proudly handed me a new one, this time a little larger than the original one.

Looking back, I can see that I was constantly at odds with myself over this issue because there was no one in my life to explain money and financial responsibility to me at that time.

My mother spent every penny she had, but only because we needed it on order to survive. So time marched on, I began earning more and more money, and I never saw the connection between earning, helping my mother pay for our basic necessities, and saving money for the future.

The child in your life may be confused about all of this as well. Should they spend it all, save it all for a rainy day, or come to some solution in the middle? Ongoing discussions and ones that include as many perspectives as possible are best. And remember to discuss the interest you earn on your savings, for compound interest is something that is misunderstood to this day by many adults.

Spending can be an even more joyous experience when you have saved up to make your purchase, and the discipline involved can carry over into every other area of your life. I learned this by accident when I was forced to save up for about two months in order to have enough for my new Schwinn bike. I took on jobs and did work I did not enjoy during that time because the thought of having enough to buy the bicycle was worth it to me.

To spend or to save, that is the question, and one that can serve as ongoing teaching moments for children. Use these wisely and the child or children in your life will have a more satisfying future as a result. This works!

How Much is Too Much? Giving, Donating, Tithing

Giving to others is a natural part of our lives, and may come about when you feel that you have more than enough for yourself and your family and want to share with others. Or it could be a concept you were raised with, where your family regularly gave money to those in need, donated to specific causes, and tithed a percentage of income to the church.

At some point you will want to have a discussion with the child in your life about this concept of giving to others. More than likely this will be a natural conversation that arises after your child hears you talking about or observes you with their own eyes give money to someone else without receiving anything tangible in return. Or, it could be the opposite situation where someone else gives you money and your child sees you and them as the recipients of giving in this manner.

My first experience with this came at age eight, when a neighbor squeezed a five dollar bill into my mother's hands and said "Please use this for whatever you need." We promptly walked the three blocks to the grocery store and during that walk my mother answered my questions about what had just occurred and explained that there were many kind people in the world who wanted to help people like us who did not have enough.

My next question was to the point when I asked her "When will we be able to give money to people who need it more than we do?" and her answer came quickly and with a twinkle in her eye. "Just as soon as our ship comes in."

I did not understand that idiom at the time, but I did know on that day that I would prefer being the one to give instead of the one to receive. It took me several decades to understand that being a good receiver was very important and a generous gift to the person giving to you.

There were more instances of people giving me or my mother money over the years, and when I was older and living on my own and the later on when I married, I continued to think of myself as someone who did not have enough money to share with anyone else. Occasionally I would give a dollar to someone begging on the street and on Sunday when I went to church I would always donate a dollar, using the tiny pencil and matching envelope in the back of the pew in front of me that was available for that purpose. And at some point I began adding my name to the envelope and was no longer simply an anonymous donor.

But my world was comprised of people who did not give or donate or tithe, or at least they never modeled that behavior in front of me. In fact, it was almost the opposite situation, where the people I worked with during my twenty years as a classroom teacher and more years than that as a real estate broker and appraiser were opposed to giving away their "hard earned money" to those who did not have enough. If they did give money to someone on a rare occasion, they would almost always share a commentary about "those people who want everything for free and are too lazy to work for it."

Can you imagine being surrounded by people who think and act in this way? It put me in the position of keeping it a secret when I did help someone financially, and silently wondering if that person could have earned the money they needed instead.

When I made the conscious decision to change my life completely in 2005, part of what I wanted to do was to be able to help others in need, to become a part of non-profits and charitable organizations and help them with fundraising efforts, and to serve people in any way I possibly could. Of course, I knew nothing about this and my only connection to fundraising was through a couple I lived next door to for a number of years. They took care of their grandson regularly from the time he was an infant and when I inquired about this they explained that their daughter was a fundraiser for several international charities and helped to organize formal events in Los Angeles several times a year. During these times they had agreed to help her by caring for their grandson for days at a time. They added that this work was important to all of them and that they considered it to be more of a calling than work.

This inspired me to do something similar and I was determined to get involved. Having lunch with a friend one day I found myself telling her that I was starting a new life where I would help non-profits with fund raising. You gave me a quizzical look and asked if I knew anything about this. I'm not sure where this came from, but I answered her with "No, but I am going to join some charitable organizations and the people who are already involved with fundraising and other things connected with helping others will teach me everything I need to know to get started."

Within a year of leaving the classroom and no longer working with real estate clients I had joined Rotary, an international service organization, and had begun assisting this group with fundraising in the community. Similar work with other non-profits followed. This changed my perspective on life completely, and these days I consider the work I do in this area to be a primary focus of my life. I donate regularly to a variety of causes, tithe, and share everything I am doing with the children in my life.

I would wholeheartedly encourage you to do the same and to make these experiences ones that you can have lively discussions around with the child or children in your life. When kids have an early reference to giving and donating it becomes a natural part of who they are and how their view of the world will be shaped and formed as they move into adulthood.

Why is Financial Responsibility Important?

The way to change the world is through
individual responsibility and taking
local action in your own community.
~ Jeff Bridges

Now that I've discussed what is meant by the term "financial responsibility", as well as the history of money, beliefs and values around money, and using money in today's world we are ready to move on to the bigger question of why the state of financial responsibility is so important.

Because history tells us that money represents the earlier form of exchange for goods and services, initially between two people and eventually between nations, we know that taking responsibility in this way makes the difference between enjoying the independence of being able to obtain what you need and having to rely on others to provide you with the items they may deem important for your survival.

So if we can agree here that responsibility equals independence then you are ready to move forward with why this matters in a day and age where people living in first world countries have access to more goods and services, necessities and luxuries, as well as technology and innovation than at any time in the history of the world.

Now we will dig deeper into the realms of modeling financial responsibility and a healthy respect for money for our children.

Next we will take a look at the financial personality of the child in your life to look at this topic from a more psychological perspective based on each person's core values.

Finally, we will discuss entrepreneurship, working for others, and the role basic personality traits such as extrovertism and introvertism play in the bigger picture of understanding and instilling financial responsibility and beliefs and values in the children we are close to and wish to mentor through life.

I began this section with a quote from actor and humanitarian Jeff Bridges He's a friend and neighbor in Santa Barbara and has been the national spokesperson for a group called "No Kid Hungry." Even though Santa Barbara is one of the wealthiest counties in California, there are still thousands of families who have difficulty feeding their children.

This situation is exacerbated during the summer months when the kids are out of school and not receiving free or reduced price lunches at school. Jeff saw a need and proclaimed that his goal was to make Santa Barbara County the first "No Kid Hungry" county in the state. He started the End Hunger Network, called in favors from some other high profile Santa Barbara residents, and as of this writing has continued to be a part of the solution to this problem. Politicians, non-profits, and regular people like me take part in a variety of activities, programs, and fundraisers to make sure as many children and families as possible have enough food to eat every day of the year. This is an example of how financial responsibility coupled with human awareness can work together to serve the people of our world.

Raising Financially Responsible Children

Respecting the Almighty Dollar

We teach our kids to respect themselves, their parents and siblings and other people in their lives, and even the family pets, but we seldom think about money as being something that must also be respected. This can be taught by lesson and by example in our quest to raise children who are financially aware and responsible.

Money is an essential part of life, and it is never too early to teach your children its value and the importance of saving, so they will be equipped to spend sensibly when they grow up. Learning the principles of responsible handling of money should give them many opportunities for advancement when they are older, which is why it is essential that, even at a young age, children cultivate a respect for money.

This shift in thinking, from one of only teaching respect in regards to humans and other living creatures to one where inanimate objects, such as toys and other belongings, as well as concepts, such as money and property are also held in high regard and respected at all times is one that requires guidance and goes into the realm of higher level and critical thinking skills. It's worthwhile in terms of teaching values and awareness that foster an understanding of deeper thoughts and ideas and can lead to early leadership qualities in the child or children in our lives that will multiply exponentially over a lifetime.

Steve Jobs used to talk about how his mother encouraged him to pursue abstract thoughts and thinking that lead to his innovative inventions at an early age. Instead of limiting him to pursuing knowledge in the areas that were already in the mainstream while he was coming of age in the 1960s and early 1970s, Jobs' mother would engage with him to help draw out his futuristic vision of the world around him. This is an example of what I am talking about here.

Money is an abstract idea in concrete form. You can hold currency, checks, and credit cards in your hands, but what they are capable of providing in our lives is more complex and subject to the interpretation of those around us. When I took a three thousand dollar cash advance on my BankAmericard in 1985 so that I could use that money as a down payment on a house I was purchasing, not to live in but as an investment, that money held the promise of what was to come to fruition at some point in the future.

To help your children understand the value of and emotions surrounding money, you might want to share the following analogy with your son that I share with many students: Money is like an accelerator (gas pedal) in a car; the amount you save and manage is similar to the amount of pressure you can apply to your own financial accelerator. Good money management affects the speed as to how quickly you are able to reach your goals. The more you save and manage, the faster you will get what you want in life.

Money can also represent an emotional experience for us, beginning in childhood. Whether a child earns the money through completing chores or other tasks or is given the money by an adult in their life, what occurs next is based on how the money makes them feel and the emotion surrounding it. When I earned money to help my mother with household expenses at eleven and twelve years old, there was deep emotion tied to it that followed me into my adult years.

This can all be traced back to respect, and how the more we respect every penny we come in contact with the more in tune we will be with our thoughts, feelings, beliefs, and values about ourselves, other people, and the world as it will unfold to us over our lifetime. Begin this practice when the child in your life is still too young to question or understand the difference and you will have a better chance of them respecting money in a way that will lead to financial responsibility at a young age. Just as we teach kids to brush their teeth morning and night, look each way before crossing the street, and to make sure the family dog has water in their bowl, the financially responsible child who has a healthy respect for money will think twice before engaging in a wasteful act with even a quarter. Once they are fully engaged with the idea of thinking of money as a tool, a concept, and something worthy of great respect if we are to enjoy its maximum benefit, children will have reached a level of thinking that many adults are never able to do, all based on how we, as the adults in their lives present the experiences and examples necessary for that type of transformational change to occur.

Teaching by Example

We all learn much more by example than by words. What I mean by this is that someone's actions can speak a thousand words while what they say out loud may be quickly forgotten.

Think back to something you observed as a child in your family growing up. What was something you remember your father or mother doing that made you think differently of them forever, whether it was positive or negative? These memories shape who we are much more than we give them credit for doing, even decades later.

I will share my own experiences of what I recall in the area of money and financial responsibility from my own childhood with you here now.

When I was five years old I used to go bowling with my father every Saturday afternoon. My parents had divorced two years earlier and this was a way for me to get to know my father and spend some time with him. It was just the two of us on these outings and I loved having him all to myself in this way.

On the way home from one of these outings we stopped at the corner market to pick up something my mother had asked him to bring home with us on our way back home. I do not recall what it was he purchased, but I do remember that the woman in line in front of us realized she didn't have enough money to pay for her entire order and was attempting to figure out what she could put back. She had a little boy with her, younger than me and he stuck his tongue out at me when I looked at him.

My father rushed forward and offered her some money. He had pulled some wadded up bills out of his pants pocket and they sat there in the palm of his open hand. The woman pushed his hand away at first, but then thanked him and took the money. Then it was our turn and after that we walked back to where my mother and I lived, without mentioning what had just happened. I also never shared this story with my mother as long as she lived.

My father's small act of kindness and compassion towards this strange woman and her child spoke thousands of words to me at my tender age. I was already old enough to know that my mother and I did not have enough money to pay for the basic necessities of food, rent, and clothing on a regular basis. I also knew that my father was not giving us any money to help out. When he gave a few dollars to someone he did not know that meant to me that other children were more important to him than I was and that he did have extra money that he could have given to us.

Can you imagine the burden of sadness that filled my heart and mind on that day? And who knows what the real story was around this incident. Perhaps he gave her his last few dollars because he felt like it was the right thing to do. And just maybe he did not give us any money because my mother did not want him to know she needed it.

The psychology around this topic is enough to send everyone to the couch for therapy for a lifetime!

Instead of allowing anything so dramatic to happen with your children, lead by example and turn one action into thousands of words as you openly discuss what is going on with the family's finances, to the degree and extent you as the adult and the other responsible adults in the household are comfortable in discussing with the children under your roof.

And using other people's situations as examples can lead into valuable discussions at your house. I have experienced this when it comes to giving, or not giving allowances, paying college tuition and expenses, and working part-time while still in high school.

If a friend is receiving twenty dollars a week in allowance at age ten, without being required to do any chores or perform at a certain level in academic and other activities, is this the right thing to emulate when it comes to your ten year old? Allow the conversation to unfold naturally and explain that you would like their input as you make your final decision as to what will work best for the family's values, goals, and beliefs. Let your child know that you value their thoughts on this and want the best for them at all times. But stand firm in your own beliefs as those you wish to utilize in your home.

When the neighbors have a party to celebrate their oldest child being accepted at their first choice college and announce they will be paying all of the related expenses during all four years, what does your family think about this arrangement? Will hearing this news from your neighbors lead to you altering the plans you have, now or in the future?

And when your sixteen year old comes home one day and asks if they may work at the fish and chips place in the food court at the mall, what is your first reaction? When they add that they have already accepted the job and will begin work later that evening, what do you do now?

Leading and teaching by example means that you will have already had a discussion around these topics and situations before they arise at your house. Knowing what others are doing is an excellent way to open your lines of communication with the other adults, as well as the kids in your life for more meaningful outcomes and superior results.

Money and Discipline

From the time I was a little girl I did not like the sound of the word "discipline." When someone said it out loud, whether it was directed at or about me or not, I would cringe and lower my eyes. In my way of thinking, discipline was going to be physically or emotionally painful, and sometimes both.

I was not disciplined by spanking as a child, but my mother did slap me on the thigh a few times for behavior that was inappropriate or unacceptable. That ended by the time I was eight or nine because I finally learned what not to do. But this was not what I thought of as discipline while I was growing up. For me that word was reserved for things that had to be done, whether I wanted to do them or not. It was the exact opposite of freedom and fun, in my opinion back then.

When first working as a residential real estate appraiser during the 1980s a woman in our office used to talk about disciplining her cat. She was very serious, and this involved getting the cat on a strict schedule of eating and sleeping. Again, I cringed. But this time her words reverberated through my mind and I wondered if she wasn't on to something that could help many people.

These days I crave the discipline I have set forth in my own life. Adhering to this disciplined behavior allows me the freedom to live where and how I choose. And these days, instead of cringing when someone talks about discipline I jump into the conversation to learn from them and to share how this works for me.

Having discipline around money and finances makes it possible to enjoy a lifestyle few can pull off because you are experiencing a heightened awareness at all times when it comes to earning, saving, spending, and giving. Allow me to explain what I mean here.

I own my own business and work as an online marketing strategist and consultant. Also, I've authored more than a dozen bestselling books on various topics related to entrepreneurship. Every day I focus on the income producing activities that I must do in order to receive money. This includes writing, marketing, creating products and courses, and mentoring and consulting with individuals and corporations. With this top of mind for several hours on the four or five days each week I work, and playing in the background during the remainder of my time, I know that this structured discipline will lead to increased income over time.

When it comes to spending, I have become more frugal than I ever thought possible. My friends will tease me about being "cheap", but the truth is that I enjoy using coupons and seeking out discounts. The challenge of finding the highest quality at the best price is one I will never grow weary of pursuing.

Giving is an easy one for me, as I have several groups and organizations where I donate and tithe a percentage of my income each year. Some of these may change from year to year, while others remain the same.

Saving and investing is a bit more complicated in my case, as I prefer to pay down real estate loans instead of saving additional income. With the help of several tax and investment experts and specialists I am at a place that is comfortable for me and my family. I'm a bit more conservative in this area as I get older, but still consider myself to be more of a risk taker than the many of my risk-averse friends and relatives.

This type of day in and day out discipline allows me to be more spontaneous than I could ever be when I was working at a job and not able to have any control over what I earned. It's fun to take an unplanned trip or purchase a luxury item or to provide this for close friends and family members from time to time. Each time I do something like this I say "Thank you, God" for the ability to do what I want to do the majority of the time. The children in my life have seen and heard the thinking behind these actions during their daily lives and it is a regular topic of discussion. And when one of them has a question or an idea that leads to me or another adult in the family taking a different action, we all celebrate this as a win.

Think of discipline in your financial affairs as the path to freedom. Before you make any decision regarding earning, spending, giving, saving, or investing ask yourself how you could accomplish the same goal in a smarter and more lucrative way. Maintain an abundance mindset at all times.

Engage experts and specialists to help educate you as to what is possible. A half of a percentage point saved on a home or car loan is huge over time. Going to the movies earlier in the day and purchasing the larger size of a food item will also add up to massive savings over time.

Recently I heard about how a young couple, still in their twenties was able to pay off college loans and credit card debt in less than four years by changing some things in their lives that were obvious to them and ignored by most people. When I first heard this story I recognized these young people as being disciplined now so they will prosper for the remainder of their lives. Let money and discipline go hand in hand and you will have much to show for it in the long run.

Your Child's
"Money Personality"

Kids and Money - Your Child's "Money Personality"

All of us are unique individuals with our own beliefs, experiences, strengths, and interests. And just as one person may be interested in baseball or rock climbing, another prefers board games and reading mysteries. Your child and the other children in your life will also have their own personality when it comes to money and financial issues.

As one of the caring adults in this child's life, it is your goal to observe, ask questions, and offer experiences that will draw out their money personality over time. Here are some questions to ask as you make your initial observations:

Does this child have an outgoing personality, or are they more reserved?

Have they exhibited a keen interest in money and finances from an early age, or do they seem to just take money for granted?

If this child wishes to have a new material item or to go somewhere that requires spending money, do they take an active role in earning the money needed or do they wait for someone else to take the lead?

Now ask your child these questions:

I see that you would like to have this new toy (or other item). How will you procure the money to make this purchase?

You have stated that you would like to have a car when you are old enough to drive. How will this car, and the related expenses of insurance, fuel, and maintenance be paid for?

Use the same speaking style and level of vocabulary that you typically would with your child on any topic when discussing important matters with them. Be prepared to wait for their answers, as you may well be the first person in their life to ask such things.

Discuss topics around money using examples from stories, movies, or current events. Make every effort to steer clear of examples from family and friends, as you may be seen as judgmental if you do so and that will detract from the experience you are trying to use as a learning moment.

Many children are extroverts and very outgoing from a young age. These tend to be the ones who enjoy selling cookies or magazines to people they hardly know. They are also more likely to set up a lemonade stand with friends and take a leadership role when it comes to business.

We must not exclude everyone else from the equation when it comes to having a "money personality" and an innate sense of all things financial. Most bankers and accountants tend to be introverts and more reserved with their actions. And stereotypes do not describe the people in our lives because human beings are three dimensional and can never be labeled accurately, nor would we want them to be.

I am simply suggesting here that you get to know the child or children in your life in a way you may not have thought about in the past, and to play the role of a financial mentor when it comes to teaching and offering experiences that will be of great value to them in the future.

Here is an example from my own life experience with two children in my life who are now young adults:

Fran was a shy, introverted child who did not seem to give a thought to money or finances when I met her at the age of ten. Her parents provided most items she wanted, and if they did not have the money or did not wish to spend it on something she asked for had no problem telling her so. When she was almost twelve her school sponsored a fundraiser by selling holiday gift wrap and other accessories to the community.

The top prize was a bicycle and Fran very much wanted to win. It was the exact bike her parents had refused to buy for her because of its cost. Fran and I had a discussion about this, and with her parent's permission I showed her how to make many sales without having to talk to many people. The strategy involved connecting with the influencers at the workplaces of her mother and father, as well as at their church and a recreation center they often visited in a nearby city. Even her grandparents and some distant cousins became a part of her sales team and were anxious to help her succeed.

Fran had five serious conversations with the right people and a month later was announced as the winner of her school's fundraising contest. Her confidence and self-esteem were at an all time high, and her school's principal even asked her to share her story in the school newspaper. I'll never forget seeing her ride down the block on her shiny new bicycle.

Alexander was an outgoing child who never met a stranger. When he discovered money and what it could be used for when he was about five he became slightly obsessed with accumulating as much of it as possible. The only issue was that he refused to spend a dime, even on something he truly wanted to have.

One day when he was about ten I had a serious conversation with him about his savings habits. It turned out that he had overheard his father and uncle talking about business and expressing concern they would have to close their doors and look for jobs if the situation did not change. Alexander had interpreted this to mean that money was tight and that he should take on the role of backup provider for the family. I then arranged a meeting with his father and explained the situation.

After Alexander spoke with his father and voiced his beliefs and concern around this situation his father reassured him that the family would be alright and that things were already looking up. He also explained that ups and downs in his business were normal and encouraged his son to come to him directly if anything was bothering him again. Then he made Alexander promise to spend and donate some of his savings and promised to begin teaching him about investing as well.

Who Is This Little Person?

I was a young stepmother and my stepson and stepdaughter were still in elementary school while I was attending UCLA and working on my undergraduate degree. Matthew was eleven years old and in the sixth grade during the quarter I enrolled in economics and one afternoon he was looking through my textbook and had some questions for me about this subject.

What ensued over the next hour was a discussion about supply and demand, stocks and bonds, and commodities. When I told him that his father and I had invested in coffee futures because of the severe rainfall in Brazil the previous season he raised his eyebrows at me and wanted to know more.

Even at this young age, Matthew already had some strong opinions about money and investing. I had no idea about this and we had never discussed this, individually or as a family. He wanted to know if we were investing money that could be lost, and if this could mean that we wouldn't have a place to live or food to eat. When I tried to assure him that his father and I knew what we were doing and that he and his sister would always be provided for, he was then curious about his college education and his future. I remember thinking at the time "Who is this little person?" You help raise a child since they are in diapers and one day they are worried about their financial future.

At this point my husband came home from work and listened for just a couple of minutes before jumping in. He dismissed Matthew to his room telling him that this was not a subject suitable for little boys and girls (nine year old Amanda was now in the room) and that they should trust us to do what was best for them. I did not say a word and my husband and I never discussed what had happened. What could have been an excellent teaching moment and the beginning of an ongoing discussion around money, investing, and financial responsibility was destroyed in that moment, and it wouldn't be for five more years, when my husband died and I became a single parent of two teenagers that the conversation would be opened up again. These days Matthew and I are business partners in several ventures, so the damage done back then was not permanent, but it certainly wasn't handled as it could have been in that moment.

But after that day I thought about money differently in regards to it being a family conversation. I started including the kids whenever possible, taking them to the bank with me and writing out the checks for our bills at the kitchen table while they were sitting beside me and doing homework. It turned out that my stepdaughter was very sharp when it came to mathematics and critical thinking, but because she was shy and an introvert I had not been aware of or given her credit for these skills and gifts. It was a slow process over the years, but the three of us learned to trust each other when it came to finances. My husband chose to be excluded from all of this, because his upbringing had dictated that children were not to be included in adult conversations, issues, or matters that were in this area of financial decision making.

So, who is this little person in your life you want to teach about financial responsibility? Whether it is your own child or

48

children or those belonging to a friend or neighbor, get the conversation moving in a forward direction. It is my personal opinion that most everything in our world these days is either financial, political, or both, including the weather, public education, or the prices of produce at the local grocery store. Discussions about anything and everything can only serve to increase awareness and to let kids know that they will have a say about their world on a regular basis. Lively discussions, based on facts and detailed information creates adults who are knowledgeable about the people of the world and the issues that will continue to unfold over their lifetimes, and do not hesitate to ask the right questions and demand some answers.

Imagine having mature conversations about the need to bring clean water to everyone in the world, education for boys and girls alike in third world countries, and the importance of eradicating diseases like polio in the last endemic countries with people who are still too short to ride roller coasters and too young to watch a PG-13 movie without permission. That's a world that will lead to more change and opportunity for everyone.

Nurturing Your Child's Beliefs and Values

I define the concept of morals and values as being "what you do when no one else is watching." We all tend to want the children in our life to share the ethics, values, and beliefs that are similar to ours, and to do the right thing when they are alone or with others. But perhaps a more healthy way of thinking about this is to educate children about some of the possible ways of thinking about their lives and encouraging them from an early age to develop their own set of beliefs and values. This helps to ensure that we are raising thoughtful thinkers and leaders who will make decisions based on what they deem to be important and feel should be a part of their lives.

Our focus here is on the beliefs and values around money, and this topic is no different than any other, I believe. We teach values and beliefs to the kids in our life every single minute of every day. And the way children learn these values is by observing what the adults around them do, and then drawing conclusions about what you think is important in life.

Regardless of what you consciously teach them, the children in your life will emerge from childhood with very clear views on what their parents and other significant adults really value when it comes to money, and with a well developed value system of their own around money and finances. And even though peers and the media can be quite influential when it comes to instilling values in kids, when all is said and done it's the adults who spend the most time with a child during their formative years that have the greatest impact throughout adult life.

Now this does not mean that you must think and plan out every word you say and action you take around finances when your children are watching. No, not at all, and in fact it's almost the opposite of this behavior you want to adopt. Act naturally, knowing that what you say or don't say and how to react to and behave around money issues is what you are passing on to those around you.

I can remember being downtown with my mother when I was about eight years old. We were doing some shopping and a small tape recorder in the window of a store caught my eye. We went inside and the salesman demonstrated how the tape recorder worked. I did not get that item on that day, but the lessons I learned from watching my mother interact with the salesman and with me during the ten minutes we spent inside the store would last a lifetime.

I came to understand that not having enough money was a topic that embarrassed my mother, and that she would say or do anything to keep from having this occur. I also saw her as being more compassionate than I had observed in the past. When we got home that night she gave me a quarter to save towards the purchase of the tape recorder I so desperately wanted, and it took me more than a month to save up the ten dollars I needed to be able to buy it. This money came from helping neighbors with a variety of chores, as well as from asking my mother for a quarter here and there that I saved instead of spending. When we took the bus downtown to buy the tape recorder about six weeks later, I was a different child because of the lessons I had learned and the beliefs and values I now held. And instead of becoming an adult who was constantly embarrassed by lack of money, I was determined to earn enough money to purchase the things I wanted and needed and to share what I had with others as well.

Perhaps taking an honest look at yourself when it comes to your beliefs and values around money is the very best course of action to take right now, for whatever money values and beliefs you hold will be the ones you are passing on to the kids in your life every minute of every day.

And again, remember that it is more important to raise a child who can think and evaluate the world around them than it is to raise someone who copies our beliefs and values without thinking or asking questions about what feels right for them in a given situation.

Entrepreneurship versus Working for Others

Introverts, Extroverts, Leaders, and Followers

When I first decided to tackle this topic of financial responsibility, beliefs, and values around money in children I made a short outline of exactly what I wanted to share. At the top of this document was all kinds of information about entrepreneurship and how this was the path to success for the child in your life.

Then I took a step back and allowed myself twenty-four hours to ponder this decision more clearly and hopefully a little more rationally. I came to the conclusion that entrepreneurship is not a part of the "right" journey towards instilling financial responsibility and values around money in the child or children in your life. Just as I discussed in chapter five, *The Financial Personality of the Child in Your Life* everyone is a unique individual and must be treated as such. This was an example of me attempting to imprint what has worked for me on you so that you would seek to emulate it. My apologies in advance if I go off on a tangent later on about the world of entrepreneurship as being superior to any other life journey in the working world.

Humans fall into many categories when it comes to basic traits, and here we will discuss introverts, extroverts, leaders, and followers. Of course, no one possesses one hundred percent of the qualities of any of these four labels. I identify as an introvert, though on occasion I may be seen as an extrovert with the behavior I display in a specific situation. This can also change as we age. That's why the term ambivert is a better descriptor of who I am.

I will also add here that I am not a psychologist and that there are many tests that are given to determine personality type, traits, and characteristics that I will not be addressing here. If you have further interest in exploring this area I would encourage you to do so in a manner that seems suitable and appropriate for your needs. What I am sharing here is simply a way to get in touch with your child as you continue your conversation and teaching about financial responsibilities and values around money.

The terms leader and follower seem to have strong positive and negative connotations, so I include the terms helper and decision maker in my discussions. I exhibit ability with decision making at times, but feel more comfortable as a helper in most situations I encounter in my day to day life.

The reason I am introducing these terms at all is so that you can observe the child in your life to determine more about whom he or she is and to teach financial responsibility in a way that will be most meaningful as this child gets older. This will also be helpful when your child is ready to go to college and/or into the work force. I know from personal experience that if you are not a good fit here your life will not be a joyous one.

Let's discuss the working world and how everything I am sharing here is connected. At some point the child in your life will be ready to take a job or start a business. This can occur at most any age, but for our purposes here let's say the child is sixteen years old and ready to enter their junior year in high school. As the responsible adult in this child's life, you know how important this experience can be. Young people are impressionable and working for someone else is very different than any interaction they have previously encountered with an adult.

Perhaps this will be a full time summer job as the front desk person for a business that provides laser tag experiences for its customers. The job entails checking people in, charging them for the time and program they are purchasing, and then directing them to the next person who will take them into the laser area.

This job pays minimum wage and the hours are from three in the afternoon until ten at night, Wednesday through Sunday with Monday and Tuesday designated as the days off.

Sounds simple, right?

Not so fast.

Your child comes home after their first day at work and head straight to their bedroom without saying a word to you. You hear the door slam and then no sound at all is emitted from their sacred space.

What do you do? Should you gently knock on their bedroom door to speak with them?

No matter what the personality type of your child, this behavior is typical. This is a teenager who has had a brand new experience over the past seven or eight hours that is unlike anything they have had in the past. Perhaps something happened at work, or maybe something happened that has nothing to do with work and is instead about friends or something else. Resist the urge to speak with them now and wait until the light of day.

The next morning's discussion and interaction is crucial in your efforts at teaching financial responsibility and instilling values around money with your child.

Let's assume they come to breakfast around eight the next morning and you sense there is a problem. Without jumping to conclusions, ask them how their first day at work went. Then wait as long as necessary for them to respond, but do insist on a response if the time is filled with an awkward silence.

No pressure here, but what you say and how you say it will impact both of you for the remainder of your lives.

Something may have happened that makes your child want to quit the job right away. Listen carefully and empathetically to make sure there has been no wrongdoing from anyone involved, and then get to the bottom of the real issue. Let them know you are on their side and believe in them.

Without getting too personal or setting up a hypothetical situation, or being judgmental, the important things to discuss at this moment are responsibility, relationships, and goals. Stick to this as your topics of the discussion and personal feelings will be seen in a different light.

I am not saying that how any of us feels is not important. Instead, I am suggesting that approaching life's more difficult moments in a logical and rational, rather than an emotional manner may have great merit, and may even have a greater impact on how serious situations will be handled in the future.

Innovators and Order Takers

In the previous chapter on understanding the financial personality of the child in your life we discussed the importance of getting to know your child more intimately before steering them towards a life that may not suit them. There are too many stories of people who claim they went into a career they did not want and set up a life not of their choosing, all because a well meaning parent or other adult led them to it over a number of years in a way that caused the child to feel like they could not step and back and stand up for themselves and were obligated to stay the course.

By getting to know your child better you will understand what type of life will be more suitable and how they can become a financially responsible, happy adult with values and beliefs that unfold naturally as a result of being exposed to many sides of issues around money since they were old enough to understand the world around them. This world starts small, when the egocentric toddler wants a toy and evolves into discussions on a global level that may eventually go over your head and beyond your realm of thinking. Now that is a joyous moment to look forward to!

During the mid 1980s while I was deciding whether to continue with my real estate career, go back to school to earn a teaching credential, or perhaps return to law school, I was at a crossroads in my life. During one summer I took a job selling cars, Toyotas more specifically, as a way to clear my mind, distance myself from the issues I was contemplating, and also earn enough income to cover my expenses. In the process I learned many things about myself and others that would become helpful throughout my lifetime.

The owner of the Toyota dealership where I worked was a man named Howard. He had been raised around cars and his uncle had owned small new and used car dealerships in the Midwest before the entire family relocated to California in the late 1950s. Howard spent as much time as possible getting to know all of his employees, including the sales people.

On one day in particular in called the sales team I was a part of into the conference room. This was upstairs and had glass walls so no matter where you were sitting at the long conference table you could see the entire sales floor. Two other teams were on duty downstairs while we were meeting with Howard that morning.

He waved his arm with a sweeping motion and asked us if we could see the members of the two teams below. We nodded yes and he asked us to just observe for a few moments to see how the sales people approached the customers who came in through any of the showroom doors. How were the sales people similar to and how were they different from one another? How were our own interactions with customers similar or different from those we were observing? Then he went around the table asking each of us why we were working there and how we thought of our role as a person selling new Toyotas.

We all had to think about that question for a moment. I was there to earn enough money to pay my bills before deciding which direction to take my life in next. I had been widowed just a year before, my step kids had decided to go back East and finish high school while living with their paternal grandparents, and I was all alone.

I honestly don't remember what the other five people on my team answered that day, but I do remember what Howard said when I told him I wasn't sure why I was there, but that I intended to do the best job I could for him and the dealership and to be a good team member.

He said, "Young lady, you have to decide right this moment whether you want to be an innovator or an order taker in life. Which will it be?"

I was taken aback but answered quickly.

"I'll be an innovator, sir."

And with that the meeting was over and Howard dismissed us to return to the sales floor in the showroom. I didn't sell even one car that day because I was preoccupied with what he had said to me.

An order taker was what someone was called who simply met with customer after customer, finding out what they wanted and needed in a car, helping arrange the financing, and delivering the car. Anyone could do this, and many times high school students even worked part-time at the dealership, as long as they were eighteen years old.

There was nothing wrong with being an order taker, and the pay was pretty good as well.

I wasn't sure what innovators did and I was too embarrassed to ask Howard what that entailed. That was a mistake on my part because I am sure he would have enjoyed sharing his thoughts and experiences on this topic with me.

When someone you like and respect offers mentoring on any level, be ready to accept the opportunity with an open mind.

But on my own I came up with a definition that worked for me during those years of my life. Innovators are the people who come up with the big ideas that order takers then help to become a reality day after day. Both of these roles have a place in our society and we must help the child in our life to choose which is right for them, before they join the work force or start a business or make another decision that will determine, at least in part the course and direction of their life.

I went back to the real estate office at the end of the summer, and by the first of the following year I enrolled in a teacher credentialing program at the local college. My goal was to be an innovator who would teach the leaders of the future.

Is the child in your life an innovator or an order taker? How can you be a part of helping them to discover their interests and exceed their potential every day? And how will an understanding of money and financial responsibility play a part in the future of this young person?

The answers to these and other questions will determine if your child will be better suited to a life as an employee or as an entrepreneur or even a small business owner. And don't rule out life as a creative, which is someone in the arts. There is room on the planet for everyone, and financial responsibility makes life a whole lot more fulfilling.

Getting Uncomfortable

Discussing careers and life paths with the child in your life may seem like fun while they are little, but I promise this won't be the case as they mature into young adults. In fact, getting uncomfortable with this subject is part of the process as you get deeper into teaching financial responsibility as a part of who they are as a human being.

Recently I attended a party put on by some good friends as we wished their daughter well on her decision to join the U.S. Marines. I have known this family for about seven years and have watched closely as this young woman has gone from being a top student and athlete in junior high to a wayward and rebellious teen during her high school years to now being anxious to serve her country and to learn more about aviation and flying helicopters while she is in the Marines for the next several years.

I have no idea what her career aspirations were when she was younger, but my guess is that this topic was not one that was emphasized during her formative years.

We cannot expect the children in our lives to come up with smart choices for themselves without the proper guidance, and time spent on this will be valuable for a lifetime. It can also be difficult at times and uncomfortable in places so we must be ready for this.

No matter what the age of your child right now, start or continue the discussion of "what do you want to be when you grow up?" This is part of the work I do with adults in my online business of teaching entrepreneurship and it's interesting how so many people from around the world find themselves looking for fulfilling and financially rewarding work they can do at their advanced age. I honestly believe that if more families would better serve their youngsters in this area my work would change in a dramatic way.

The following exercise is most appropriate for children aged nine to ten and older, in my experience. Sit down with a notebook and make some notes before bringing your child into the conversation. These are some questions to ask yourself:

- Who is my child? By this I mean what are they like when you get to know them well and spend time with them. You know your child better than anyone else does right now, so you are the most qualified to answer this question before they become adults and their true identity is altered by peers, other adults, and life situations. Dig deep here and include everything you can about what they have already encountered and dealt with in their young life.

- What are their likes and dislikes? Include things such as preferring the outdoors to being inside, choosing to read rather than going out with friends, and how they choose to spend a day off from school when given the choice to plan their own day. Even knowing if they are a morning person or not can influence their choices for work and careers over a lifetime.

- Is this child a self-starter who exhibits taking the initiative, or someone who has to be reminded several times to complete homework, care for a pet, help with chores, or handle a situation with a friend?

- Would you describe this child as being a creative thinker? Artistic? Logical? Productive? A go-getter? Organized in thought and action? Empathetic? Come up with your own list of words and phrases that make sense to you, knowing that it is difficult to do this objectively in regards to someone you love and care about so much.

- Does this person think of themselves in a positive way? What I'm referring to here is whether or not they have confidence, self-esteem, and a positive image of themselves, inside and out.

- What has this child shares in terms of what they would like to do when they are older? Where did the idea come from? Why are they making this choice for a job or a career?

You want to encourage the child or children in your life to think about their future in a way that includes work, play, friends, family, and values. By having a discussion around the topic of choosing a career path early on you will enable them to get a jump start on their future as a productive member of the work force in a capacity that suits who they are as a human being and concerned citizen.

And I will add here that it is a good thing to have two or three choices about the work this child will do as an adult as interests and circumstances can and will change over time. For example, I wanted to become a veterinarian beginning when I was about ten years old. After volunteering on the weekends at the local zoo and then working part-time in a veterinarian's office during my high school years I came to the realization that for a variety of reasons I would prefer to do something else for a living and have many pets of my own instead. Also, the work I've been doing online since 2006 did not exist before the late 1990s, so that is another factor to take into account in our fast moving world.

What If We Teach
Financial Responsibility?

Leadership is the capacity to
translate vision into reality.
~ Warren Bennis

If we begin teaching financial responsibility and values around money from an early age, everyone benefits. I found that out through my experiences as a classroom teacher in the public schools in the inner city of Los Angeles.

As a new teacher in the late 1980s I was given free rein to add appropriate lessons to any topic I was teaching. I had fifth grade those first few years and in my early discussions with the students during math time it came to light that many of them were curious about checking accounts and the writing of checks. Many of my students came from homes where no bank account had been set up so that the family could write checks for their rent, utilities, groceries, and other purchases.

They typically had a savings account at the local bank that allowed them to cash checks, but they operated primarily on a cash basis for the majority of their expenditures. If cash was not acceptable for something they wanted or needed, the bank or the post office would sell them a money order. These people had immigrated to the United States from Mexico, El Salvador, Guatemala, and Vietnam, where banking was only prevalent for the middle and upper classes.

I created a four week mathematics unit on checking accounts that was both popular and helpful to my students and their families. Using checks from my own checking account, I deleted my name and account number. Then I made copies for everyone in the class and had them start a notebook for this unit. Every morning I would add something by writing it on the board. This might be a check they received as a birthday present or from a job they did for a neighbor, or it could be a check they wrote the night before at the grocery store or at the mall. It was fun, and soon the parents got involved.

After school one afternoon each week the parents would come in to my classroom to see what we were doing. I loved watching my ten and eleven year old students help their parents and grandparents learn how to maintain and balance a checking account. My most important rule was that you could not hand someone a check you had written until you entered the information in your check register. It was too easy to forget what you had done, and my kids were adamant about passing this piece of the puzzle on to their family members.

The example I used was going to the local mall one evening, writing four checks for items at four different stores and then not being able to remember one or two of the stores or the items when you went to fill in your register the following day. You can't find the receipt and two things you bought were for friends and now you're in a big mess. It seems everyone can relate to going to the mall and buying items from more than one store, so the example was a helpful one.

My students also learned about fees and charges from the bank, what could happen if you issued a check without sufficient funds to cover it, why a check you deposited on one day may not clear your checking account until several days later, and why it was important to think about every penny you earned and spent to be a responsible adult and member of the community.

I didn't think about it at the time, but the truth was that I was involved in multi-generational financial education and could have made this one of the areas I specialized in as a teacher. This could have become a part of a much larger program that would have been taught in schools around the country to educate students and family members in this area. Instead, after spending six years at that first school I then moved on to another school where my check writing unit went by the wayside because in this new setting this content and information was not quite as relevant and appropriate to this population of students and their families. The students I taught at the second school came from middle class families who were more familiar with banking specifically and finance in general.

I assumed, and assumptions are always dangerous, that my experience with the banking system (I had worked as a merchant teller in a large commercial bank years before becoming a classroom teacher) was not needed in my new setting. Looking back, the check writing unit would have been just as important, perhaps for different reasons.

Personally, I believe that everyone can benefit from financial education, beginning even before one starts attending school formally. Understanding money, including paper and coin currencies, checking and savings accounts, and the credit and debit card system can only enhance one's knowledge of the bigger picture of financial knowledge, and any training provided could be embraced as a part of an overall education.

It is our responsibility as parents, family members, teachers, and other adult role models to start the conversation around money at an early age and to encourage questions and ongoing discussions from the children in our lives at all times. Teaching by example will continue to be the best way to enlighten our young people, and explaining why someone might use cash instead of a credit card, use an app to keep track of gas mileage, or set up an automatic payment or deposit are all excellent examples to share. Learning about money also instills a respect that will be most beneficial over time as major life decisions are made in regards to how much money might be available at the given time.

Back in the classroom I was applauded for early intervention with financial education by teaching my unit on checking accounts to fifth graders, but the truth is that my students could have already been a part of this type of training, albeit more age appropriate from the time they entered preschool or Kindergarten. With the child in your life, open up the conversation around money as early as you deem your child to be ready and then let the financial education begin!

The Financially
Aware Adult

Saying "No" When You Want to Scream "Yes!"

We want the best for our children, of course, and part of that desire includes knowing they have grown into financially aware adults. But how and when does that happen? Not by accident, and certainly not often enough unless we make that a priority within our family from when the children are at a very young age.

But in our quest to raise a financially aware adult, we do make this a priority, and with joy in our hearts I might add. Having the discipline and confidence to say no to expenses and purchases you cannot afford is a super power in today's world. Too many people live well beyond their means, and the term "keeping up with the Joneses" is all too common. This phrase is an American expression which began in 1913 with characters in a comic strip created by Arthur R. "Pop" Momand. The Joneses never actually appeared in this comic strip, but they exerted their influence in every one of the storylines. People want to keep up appearances to show others they are doing well, and everything falls apart over a very short period of time. You may have seen this occur with your friends or neighbors over the years. I certainly did, and most of the times it was not related to a downturn in the economy or anything else of that nature.

So how does one keep from buying to many things and spending more than they have? My answer should be obvious by now; this feat is accomplished by going back to the lessons, values, beliefs, and traditions one was raised with, assuming there was a caring adult who made sure this was a part of the regular routine with the children they were surrounded by during their formative years.

I believe that we become more financially responsible as we grow older simple because we have been through so much when it comes to managing our money and making financial decisions all of our adult lives. We may see something we want with all of our heart and actually have the ability to purchase, perhaps with a credit card. But we resist because we know it makes more sense not to give in to these urges. We are both responsible and aware of our financial situation. But what if we could teach the child in our life to be more financially aware, more thoughtful, and more interested in the future at a young age. Good news...we can!

Depending upon your upbringing and experience, at some point in time you knew what it was like for your parents, or the adults who were raising you to not have enough money to pay for a basic need. I've already talked about my experiences growing up in poverty, but let's take a look at some examples that are not quite as drastic and were handled differently.

My close friend grew up in the Midwest, one of five children, living with her parents, siblings, and also a cousin. Her father worked in construction and was often out of work during the winter months when it was simply too cold to be building anything or working outdoors. Her mother used to save money by putting away a few dollars here and there as she was able to during the more prosperous months. They would also purchase meat to keep in their freezer and even buy extra cans of food to store in their pantry during the other months so they would have enough to eat and to pay for the heating of their home during those bitter cold months. It was stressful at times, but they made their situation work for the family's good.

This pattern of behavior was observed and internalized by my friend even before she was a teenager, so somewhere in the back of her mind she understood the concept of saving for a rainy day. It's no wonder that her spending and saving habits have been maintained on an even keel over the years. This is possible because of the foundation that was laid while she was growing up. In all of the years we have been friends I have never known her to throw caution to the wind and spend money she didn't have. She is also a very generous person, and being financially aware allows this part of her personality to shine.

We must give the children in our life an opportunity to experience the phenomenon of not having enough money and being forced to choose between which items and obligations to pay for and which to postpone on a regular basis. You can help facilitate this by providing regular and ongoing opportunities for them to be in the position of choosing wisely.

Perhaps the choice for a ten year old is between spending every dollar they have saved for that new pair of basketball shoes and wearing the old ones a little longer while doing some extra chores or work for others to earn some additional cash. Or maybe it's the college graduate beginning a job in a new city and having to decide what type of living situation makes sense for their salary, and if having a roommate or two would be a smart option to consider for the first year or even longer.

And I'd like to point out here that the choice that is made is not quite as important as the thinking and logic that was put into making it at the time. We'll discuss this more later in this book, as it is a topic that can have lifelong ramifications in other areas of our lives as well.

Seeing the Payoff from Financial Self-Control

As we make the commitment to financial awareness and responsibility for ourselves, we must also carry that goal with us each day as we spend time with the child or children in our life. Actions speak much louder than words, so get into the habit of thinking about how you might handle a situation before it presents itself. Financial self-control is all about being willing to take charge of your emotions, being in control of the moment, and knowing that how you act today and what you are willing to sacrifice now will pay off handsomely in the future.

For example, how do you react when another driver cuts you off on the highway, someone says something uncalled for to you or to someone you are with, or when someone asks you to do something you consider to be unethical or immoral? On the financial side of this, how do you handle it when you have a bill due and do not have the money on hand, or when a client or customer owes you money and they will not pay, or when someone wants to borrow money from you?

All of these are instances when you must rely on your values and beliefs to guide you in the moment, and all require that you have an internal system that helps you to maintain self-control when you become emotional or irrational around a situation.

Financial self-control is what keeps us from making purchases we cannot truly afford, becoming financially obligated to payments that are more than we have budgeted for, and having the respect for money that it deserves as a part of our daily lives. Helping the child in our life to have this same type of attitude and ability is crucial to their adult experience and begins when they are very young. Again, look for opportunities to turn situations into "teachable moments," which are defined as the time at which learning a particular topic or idea becomes possible or easiest.

This concept of "teachable moments" has been around since the early 1900s, but was made popular and more commonplace during the 1950s in the United States by physicist, educator, and aging expert Robert Havighurst in his 1952 book, *Human Development and Education*. In this book Havighurst stated:

"A developmental task is a task which is learned at a specific point and which makes achievement of succeeding tasks possible. When the timing is right, the ability to learn a particular task will be possible. This is referred to as a "teachable moment." It is important to keep in mind that unless the time is right, learning will not occur. Hence, it is important to repeat important points whenever possible so that when a student's teachable moment occurs, he or she can benefit from the knowledge.

A teachable moment is often best demonstrated with a significant emotional or traumatic event, the emphasis being on the "moment" versus the lesson."

I believe that this is a relevant concept to introduce and discuss here and that we must incorporate the essence of this message into our interaction with the child in our live in regards to financial self-control. A well known saying from Maya Angelou comes to mind here, and that is "I've learned that people will forget what you said, people will forget what you did, but people will never forget how you made them feel." When Havighurst mentions that teachable moments can often be demonstrated best when there occurs a significant emotional or traumatic event.

Compelling yourself to exercise this type of self-control when you are in a state of mind resulting from something negative that has happened to you or to someone close to you requires that you call upon years of preparation in an instant. We have all heard of parents who exhibit super human strength when their child is in physical harm's way and people who behave in a heroic way when put to the test. This is the type of self-control I am referring to here.

When push comes to shove and the situation demands that you choose between desiring what you want at the moment and what you are sure you will need in the future, choose wisely. Swallow your pride, do what you know down deep inside of you is the right thing, and allow the child in your life to observe this behavior and the chain of events up close. Voice your thoughts and encourage questions and comments as you deem appropriate to the situation. These are the life lessons and the memories that turn good kids into future thought leaders.

Living Within Your Means

Although living within your means is not as difficult as most people make it out to be, I will admit this has been an ongoing challenge for me as an adult. It takes some discipline to make the necessary changes but I can say from personal experience it will be well worth the effort. At the very least, you will be able to sleep much better each night knowing you aren't burdened with debt and financial obligations that are out of control.

If you have struggled with excessive debt at any time in your adult life, especially credit card debt, you know that destroying the card cards and closing the accounts is an excellent option to consider. This is the surest way to make sure you don't get yourself into trouble with spending more than you make and once you do this you see that having just one credit card for travel and specific expenses and paying it off each month, and using a debit card for everything else makes sense.

I wrote earlier about trying to "keep up with the Joneses." In a culture where almost everyone can buy or lease the latest luxury vehicle or a new sports car, and having the latest and greatest new technology feels like a right rather than a privilege doesn't mean you need to follow suit. There is something very freeing in living a more simplistic life and it is certainly less stressful.

When I built a new home in Santa Clarita, California, one of the two cities I continue to live in, it was during that first summer I went door to door collecting non-perishable food items for one of the two local food banks. I left a brown paper bag with a note explaining everything attached, and returned three days later to pick up the filled bags. I was shocked at how little had been donated until I realized that many of my neighbors were "house rich" and "cash poor" because of their lifestyle choices.

Within two years the Great Recession hit, and about a third of the homes in my neighborhood went into foreclosure. I walked up and down the streets trying to make sense of what had happened there. I came to the conclusion that those who had purchased designer furniture and high end appliances, put in pools and spas, and had luxury hardscape (this refers to stairs and patios and driveways and other items, typically constructed out of concrete or bricks) and lush, professionally designed landscape installed had not budgeted to make sure they had enough cash on hand to make their mortgage payments. On the other hand, the only new furniture I purchased during that time was a badly needed mattress and bedroom set, and I only had grass and sprinklers installed as a requirement of the Homeowner's Association. My previous experiences with real estate investing made me keenly aware of the pitfalls to avoid.

I continue to hear people talk about not wanting to have to think about every dollar before they spend it or go into debt to make a purchase, but those tend to be the same people who have too much month left at the end of their money. Instead, take pride in the fact that you *are* taking the time to think about expenditures and know that you will always have a little extra, even when there are unforeseen emergencies.

Explaining these concepts to the child in your life can be beneficial on many levels. Be open to their questions and comments, as these may spark an idea you had not thought of or give you the chance to explain something you have done for years and take for granted in a way that opens your mind to new possibilities. This type of communication around financial responsibility and values is priceless.

A Limitless Future

Yes, I Can Afford That

Financially confident young adults are very appealing to employers, banks, organizations, and also other young adults who have that level of maturity. And contrary to popular belief, these people are fun to spend time with and generous with their time and giving to others, in my experience.

If you have put in the time and made the effort on a regular basis to educate your child about money, beliefs, and values in a way that makes sense for you and for them, when they come of age and are ready to move on to their next life experience it will be a joyous moment. This young person will be a leader among their peers and ready to take on new and exciting challenges. This is a proud moment for both of you and one you will both cherish for a lifetime.

At some point they will come to you and announce they are considering taking action in a direction that requires thought, research, an evaluation of their current situation, and most importantly, money. If they are coming to you in advance of making their decision, give yourself an additional pat on the back for building a relationship based on honesty, openness, and trust. Once a child turns eighteen they know they do not need your permission, but knowing they value your opinion and want to discuss the details with you is an excellent way for them to begin their life journey as an adult knowing they have you, and perhaps other adult family members in their corner. After your initial conversation it's nice to hear them say, "Yes, I can afford that!" in regards to their goal.

This goal could be to spend a year abroad, working or in school, to relocate to a new city, to purchase a first home, to buy a new car, or to pursue a graduate degree in an area of interest to them. You will be there not only to cheer them on, but also to mentor them as to the details and other things they must take into consideration before moving forward. How fun it is to plan in this way with your now adult child. They are not your friend, and you want to maintain those boundaries, but the relationship will have shifted ever so slightly as they are recognized and acknowledged as the head of their own household.

Allow them to take the lead, and do not be afraid to tell them what you really think. Perhaps they are wishing to combine two or three goals into a single transaction, such as buying a new car and taking a new job in a new city in another state. This could signal disaster, as too many "new" things may also have psychological implications and repercussions down the road. If you get the feeling they could be entering into entanglements that would not be so easy to unwind, speak honestly with them about your concerns and suggest an alternate route to the same goal destination.

This is also the time to remind them of your teachings around financial responsibility of years past, where being able to afford something does not necessarily mean it's the right path to go down at this time. This is also the time when you casually slide back into your role as parent, other family member, adult role model, or other position you have held over the years and talk to this young person in a way that shows you care about them much more than about money. I believe everyone needs to be reminded of this, especially when making significant life decisions that could alter the course of a life.

And if this new goal makes sense when discussed out loud, this will be a time to celebrate with other family members, old friends, and new colleagues. When you can afford to make decisions based on solid thinking and planning, it's a celebratory moment. The new car or home, relocating to a new city, returning to school to earn a graduate degree, or anything else is something to be memorialized and commemorated to signify your trust and belief in their decision as someone who has made the successful transition from child into young adult.

Just imagine how different your life might have been if you had had a special adult to guide and mentor you in this way since you were a little child? And if you were fortunate to have this type of upbringing and ongoing mentoring, take a moment now to thank that person and tell them how grateful you will always be for what they did for you.

Being Prepared for a Rainy Day

For those who are not financially responsible, they see no need to prepare for a rainy day. Why is this so? It's because for them every day is not only a rainy day, it's a torrential downpour! Instead of going into debt for stylish galoshes, a matching rain slicker, and a fancy umbrella from a popular designer, it's best to be financially responsible and prepared in advance for the inevitable situations and circumstances that are simply a part of everyday life.

Once when I was on my way to speak at an event in Las Vegas, a five hour drive from where I live in southern California I got a flat tire. It was during the winter months when it became dark before six o'clock and I was driving alone in my car. This occurred around seven in the evening in Zzyzx, California near the Zzyzx Road exit on Interstate 15, in the middle of the Mojave Desert and one hundred miles southwest of my destination in Las Vegas. This location is pretty much in the middle of nowhere. As I used my cell phone to call AAA I thought about my predicament.

Here I was, sitting alone in my car in the dark, and although I had someone coming to help me I was afraid I would not recognize the tow truck when it arrived and might mistakenly open up my car door or window to a stranger. I tried turning on the interior car lights, but still couldn't see who was approaching. I finally decided to call a friend to have someone stay on the line with me until help arrived, but it was a Friday night and I couldn't reach anyone. I decided not to leave any messages that might not be picked up for hours and did not want to worry anyone needlessly, so I hung up and waited. With cars and trucks flying by me at excessive speeds I knew I had not prepared myself for this moment when I knew better.

This situation turned out fine and within an hour I was on my way to my destination with a "donut", what we call our "limited use, space saving" spare tire securely mounted on the front left of my car. Those are only good for a limited number of miles, so now I also needed to purchase a tire in Las Vegas before driving back to California three days later.

Upon arriving at my hotel, I got settled into my room and then made a list of what I needed to do to be better prepared for this type of situation in the future. This included not driving alone in the dark so far from home ever again, having one or two people to check in with while I was on this type of trip, and looking into getting a full size spare tire for the future. Also, I wrote down what I had done properly to prepare, including always driving a late model vehicle, having it checked out by a mechanic less than a week before leaving on the trip, and having a AAA "Plus" membership that offered up to one hundred miles of free towing, free fuel and fuel delivery, and lockout service. This package is only about thirty dollars a year more than the basic service but could really come in handy at times like I'm describing here.

Within days of getting back home I used my checklist to implement what I had suggested for future occasions and congratulated myself on now being more responsible. And when I decided to take a twenty-one day, sixty-three hundred mile road trip through seventeen states all by myself a few years later, I was thankful for the previous experience and the opportunity to become more prepared.

Financial preparedness includes having at least six months of living expenses on hand, something few people seem to have. It's much more appealing to many to buy more stuff and do more things rather than to prepare for a rainy day and then move forward confidently in your daily life.

As a mentor to the child in your life, discuss these concepts with them so they will have the advantage of being prepared as fully as possible for what might occur in their life.

Making Choices Based on Financial Preparedness

The most fun part of growing up is having the ability to make choices without consulting a parent or other adult figure. I can still remember how it felt when I was first choosing what and when to eat, what to do on a day off, and how to keep house in my first apartment. I ate canned ravioli for dinner and breakfast one time, heating it up in my little sauce pan. I decided to sleep until nine and then go to the mall on my day off. And I didn't make my bed at all the first week. I was a grown up now and the only person I was beholden to was my boss. Or so I thought.

After that first week of being on my own my beliefs and values kicked in. I could hear the little voices in my head from my mother, friends, and other adults who were a part of my life at that time. The next morning I made my bed. At first, these voices were around responsibility in general. That evening I prepared a proper dinner for myself and ate it from a plate while sitting at my kitchen table. Then, slowly these voices were shouting at me for not being financially responsible.

I was working as a waitress at this time, and even though it paid less than minimum wage, something that was allowed at that time if you had the possibility of earning tips, I did earn lots of money in tips and had cash on hand at all times. When this is what you get used to, you see money as almost being disposable. Spend a few dollars, earn a few more dollars. It's this mentality that can keep you broke and without a financial plan to work out for yourself.

So I heeded the voices of those I respected that were swirling around in my head, and by the second week everything had changed. I made the decision to return to college in the fall and to let Al, the owner of the restaurant I was working in at that time know about my plans. Instead of being afraid to share this type of information with him because I thought he would judge me or even let me go before the summer was over, make an attempt to talk me out of it, or otherwise make me feel uncomfortable, I waited until the slow part of the afternoon and told him I wanted to speak with him about something. He raised his eyebrows at me and then we sat down at an empty table in the back of the restaurant. He stretched out his hand as a signal for me to begin the conversation.

As my words spilled out, probably faster and much less organized than I had planned, Al just listened patiently until I finished. Then he said something I will never forget.

"I was hoping you wouldn't work here forever. You're smart and people like you. Go back to college and make something of yourself. If you wait too long, it'll be too late."

I didn't ask him to explain. I don't think I even thanked him for saying nice things about me. But I did nod and smile as we both got up from the table. Then I went into the bathroom and cried. Al was a relative stranger to me, as I had only been working at the restaurant for about a month. And this stranger, this man who could be tough and demanding and seemed to never smile believed in my ability and potential to be something more than I was right then.

For the remainder of that summer I saved half of what I earned. I loved seeing the numbers grow in my savings account book. I became more conscientious of my work habits. I continued to make my bed every day. And I like to think I matured a little bit because of it. When I returned to college I was prepared financially. I was also a more serious student after that experience.

When you have laid the groundwork and given your life some thought, the final step is financial preparedness. It's like having an angel watching over you in that you know what you can do on your own and what you might need to ask for help with in order to achieve. During that year I purchased a new car and my first home, in that order. I needed the car to get to the part-time job I had taken across town. That job made it possible to get the loan for the house.

Being prepared financially has its rewards and I was ready to receive them. Teach this to the child in your life and they will receive rewards throughout their lifetime. It's a gift that keeps on giving.

How Do You Teach Financial Responsibility?

Luck is where preparation meets opportunity.
~ Seneca

I've discussed what is meant by financial responsibility, why it is so important to provide your child with a financial education, and the "what ifs" of incorporating this conversation into our daily lives as early as possible as we interact with our children. But how exactly do you teach these concepts, methods, strategies, beliefs, and values to another human being?

My thoughts and beliefs here are strong ones that I have spent over half a century refining and fine tuning. Of course, it is not my intention to either overtly or covertly persuade you to my side, but instead to guide you to creating your own handbook of values, beliefs, and conclusions that make sense for you and your family.

It is my precept that everyone learns by lessons, examples, discussions, and recalculation. This is similar to the Socratic Method, where individuals engage is a rigorous type of cooperative argumentative dialogue. My method is based on asking and answering questions that will stimulate critical thinking and also draw out ideas of importance and underlying presumptions, so my simplified variation is not intended to be in any way derivative in nature.

Instead, I have come up with a process that is more similar to a lesson plan. My twenty years of formal classroom teaching in the inner city of Los Angeles led me to pursue a method that would incorporate something commonly referred to in education as a "seven step lesson plan" to make sense of and get results from the children who passed through my doors. I began to experiment with my own family members and the children of close friends and the outcomes began to speak for themselves. Allow me to explain.

The discussion begins with the adult presenting the topic of the lesson to the child. One on one instruction works best but I have also experienced success when using this method in small groups of no more than five children working with one adult. In the classroom I simply broke up the children into groups of four or five and went from group to group to deliver the lesson in the way I had planned.

Let's say our lesson that day is on spending money. Do not add an adverb modifier, such as spending money wisely or spending money frivolously, as these tend to be viewed as judgments on the part of the adult role model that will cloud the lesson and thus, diminish its value. Present the lesson in a straightforward manner, allowing the child or children to come to their own conclusions on what is right or wrong, and what lies in the gray area. Provide as much information and resource material as possible while still keeping it relevant to your topic.

Next come the examples, where characters are created to model the thinking, behavior, and results of someone in a specific type of situation. Perhaps the character spends their lunch money on snacks at the local convenience store on their way to school, is then unable to purchase lunch, and the result is a headache that requires them to visit the nurse's office and miss their fifth period English class.

You guide the discussion, but allow the child to voice their thoughts and opinions openly before entering into the conversation to add your own. At some point you will finally express your own thoughts and opinions, being careful to limit your words to those that are appropriate and necessary.

Remember here that your actions will always speak louder than your words and that even the slightest shift in body language can have profound effects on children for many years to come.

Recalculation involves allowing time to think about the lesson and the examples and this is best achieved when the child is given quiet time alone to write down their experience, questions, and conclusions of what you have presented. This silence speaks volumes on how the young mind can make sense of the world around them and develop their own character and values on a topic they may have seldom thought about in the past.

This strategy is effective on any topic you can think of and I have used this with children of all ages to discuss topics as serious as drinking and driving and as playful as grooming a domestic pet. This method of introducing a topic and then using lessons, examples, discussions, and recalculation allows for a vigorous and animated learning experience in which everyone is involved and ultimately benefits from what transpires.

What I am sharing here is not intended to ever persuade or manipulate someone to another's way of thinking, but merely to enhance the learning process in a fair and democratic way. Exposing the child in your life to what I have outlined here will only enhance their life experience and make for more financially aware and responsible adults.

Allowances and Earning Income

My Allowance, Please

You may have noticed that I have waited until now to discuss the topic of allowance. There is a good reason for that and I will share it with you. My feelings about giving a child an allowance have changed and shifted significantly over the years, based on a variety of factors including, but not limited to my observations of many kids and their families, my own experiences with this model, and the numerous children and adults I have discussed this with over at least the past twenty-five years. I will state upfront that I do not believe in giving allowances to children.

There are two types of allowances I will discuss here; the first one is money given to a child with no expectation of them doing anything in return and the second type requires specific behaviors in return for this money. These specific behaviors include, but are not limited to chores and work around their home or property, maintaining certain grades and scores at school, listening and following directions at home and at school, and only spending a specific amount of time looking at screens (television, video games, computers, smart phones) for a specific number of hours each day.

When you give a child money on a regular schedule without requiring them to do anything in order to "earn" it, which is typically weekly or monthly you render them helpless in developing their own ability to create an income of their own.

When you give them money and require that certain behaviors be followed, they give away their power to make decisions for themselves and force them into behaviors and actions that may be unnatural for them.

Both are poor models, in my opinion and do not lead to financial responsibility and values in the way that you want for the child in your life as they move closer to adulthood and independence on all fronts.

There are infinite studies and arguments for and against giving children an allowance, and ultimately you will do what feels right in your unique situation.

You may be wondering what I recommend instead of either of these models, and the answer is one none of us likes to hear...

It depends.

It depends upon the personality of the child in your life, taken into consideration with their current age, level of maturity, prior experience with allowances and financial education within the family, and a host of other factors, such as the values and beliefs around money within the immediate family, if they live an urban or rural lifestyle, and if they are in traditional school or are homeschooled.

My experience with receiving an allowance was an interesting one. When I was around nine or ten years old one of my girlfriends announced that she had saved up her allowance and was going to buy herself a new bicycle. She and her parents were going together to choose the one she had picked out. I had no clue what she meant.

"Allowance?" I asked. "What is this thing called allowance and how do I get one?"

She looked at me as though I was from another planet and proceeded to explain to me in great detail how she first got allowance from her parents when she was five years old, and that the amount increased every year on her birthday.

"So is it a birthday present?"

"No, you have to earn it."

"By doing what?"

"You know, being good and doing what your parents ask you to do without complaining, and doing good at school."

I went straight home and asked my mother where my allowance was and if I could have it retroactive to when I was five years old. It was as if I thought there would be a pile of money waiting for me in a shoebox or drawer, and that all I had to do was ask for it and the cash would finally be delivered to me in full. It would be like a dowry or an inheritance I had coming to me after working so hard as a child for almost a decade. How and where would I spend it all, I thought.

My mother and I sat down at the kitchen table and she explained that she had no money to give me, but that she would try to give me a dollar here and there to make up for it.

That led to me taking odd jobs around the neighborhood and taking more financial responsibility for my mother and myself, something I continued until she passed away at the age of ninety-three. And that is when I began to formulate my own thoughts and beliefs about allowance and my controversial ideas on why it is not a valuable concept to promote or engage in with anyone of any age. Yes, there are adults who receive an allowance from a parent or spouse.

Money is connected to at least one emotion in most families. It can represent power or greed or happiness or guilt or any of a host of other deep feelings and emotions, alone and in combination under varying circumstances. The important thing is to try to make every memory as positive a one for the child in your life as possible, as you would do with birthdays, holidays, and other special occasions. Controlling the purse strings in a way that makes you or your child feel awkward or alienated can and will lead to issues in adulthood that may take years of therapy to overcome. Over the years I have even encountered adults, typically younger wives who describe the money they have access to as disposable income as being an allowance from their husband. I have also known men and women who still receive an allowance from a parent as a part of a family trust. They feel it is their birth right to receive this money as regular payouts for their entire lives.

Instead of providing an allowance, whether it is performance based or just paid out without question or discussion, perhaps you will choose to have conversations about money on at least a weekly basis. And when the child in your life wants or needs a bicycle, school supplies, or other items, maybe this can be yet another opportunity to discuss some of the concepts that will lead to them becoming a financially responsible and aware adult.

Chores?! You Mean I Have to Work?

Whereas allowance sets up, in my opinion patterns of dependence upon others and the belief that we must trade hours for dollars, performing chores and offering services to others in the way I will explain and discuss here is an excellent was to learn some preliminary skills around business and entrepreneurship. Even though I was completely unaware of this at the time, my early experiences were shaping my thoughts and ideas around money in a way that benefits me to this day as an entrepreneur. Allow me to explain.

When you are "hired" to complete a specific task in return for a certain amount of money you are given choices inherent to the job; you get to decide how the work will be done, by whom, and in what time frame, with few restrictions or exceptions. This is quite different than being paid a specific amount of money per hour. The examples I will use here include my early experiences with babysitting, as well as with scraping barnacles off the sides of wooden boats, long before most boats were constructed out of fiberglass.

Earlier in the book (in Chapter Two) I described my first experiences with babysitting and how excited I was to earn money by watching and caring for the young children or family friends and neighbors. So much so, that while I was in junior high a started a babysitting business. I put together a group of five other girls and myself and formed two person teams to babysit for people who needed childcare in order to work and could not afford to pay adults or use more traditional means of childcare. I make no judgment here as to why anyone would trust an infant or toddler to be cared for by children not yet thirteen years old and of unknown character, but they needed the help and we wanted to earn money that summer.

Because I had started this business, I found the customers and made the assignments. I also took a cut of everyone else's pay and they were all fine with that. It was assumed and unspoken that the person in charge would earn more money. This put me in a position of leadership and I believe I was more than fair with everyone.

The idea I want to convey here is that I had already traded in the "dollars for hours" concept for one around the belief that by finding others to work for and under me I could cover more territory and find more customers.

I even recruited two boys from across the street to procure leads for the business and paid them five dollars for every person they brought to me that resulted in a minimum of fifty dollars in income. These guys were very creative and scoured the neighborhood on their bikes, talking to everyone who seemed like a prospect. One day they found a very little boy outside of his house all alone and took him back inside where his mother was talking on the phone. They convinced her to let my team watch him for a few hours each week so she could go shopping and talk on the phone and not have to worry about him getting into trouble or being injured or worse.

On the other hand, the job of scraping barnacles off boats was a labor intensive one that depended on being able to take the pain, excruciating at times, of using a rubber trowel to gently scrape the barnacles (these are marine crustaceans with an external shell, which attach themselves permanently to a variety of surfaces, particularly to the bottoms of wooden boats that stayed in the water all of the time) off the sides. The boat owners would pull them out of the water and on to trailers, where they would bring them home and park them in their driveway for a few days so they could be scraped and cleaned. Once you cut yourself on one of the barnacles the blood would mix with the salt water and make you cry out in pain. But the pay was good and the people always very nice, so my friends and I did this for a couple of summers until we wised up and found new ways to earn money.

Even if my mother would have had enough chores to keep me busy during the summers and at various other times throughout the year, working outside of my home just made more sense. You will have to decide whether to pay the child in your life to do chores, and if so, which ones and for how much money. Remember that everything is a learning experience and teachable moment in which you connect more deeply with your child and find out what motivates them and how they approach and handle real life situations. When children are given responsibility they either rise to the occasion or retreat. You need to know which it is and deal with this behavior as you see fit to build strong character.

In the case of the babysitting business I founded, I was surprised to discover that many girls had no interest in being involved because their allowance was sufficient for their needs (buying school clothes was important to all of us), whether or not they were asked to do anything in return for receiving this set amount of money each week.

It would have been interesting to follow up with these girls after high school or college to find out how they were handling money, but perhaps the parents were continuing with the allowance strategy even then. I did follow up with some of my fellow barnacle scrapers a few years later and we all were in agreement that we would not do that type of work ever again, for any amount of money. Then we compared our hands to see who had the worse scars. Nothing like being reminded of events from our childhoods to help shape your later years.

Independence through Personal Income

I lived in southern Florida during my teenage years, and this is where I first had friends who came from extremely wealthy families. These experiences that I went through over that period of time are now, as I look back, priceless in my life's journey.

Coming from a single parent family where we were below the poverty level throughout my childhood and meeting people who had more money than I could imagine was exciting at first and insightful over time. I had assumed that having lots of money, or even enough money would solve all of a person's problems, but of course this isn't true. But it was fun to spend time with people who lived so differently from the way my mother and I were living. I was invited to private clubs where you could order anything you wanted from a private chef and it was billed to the member at the end of the month. Without judging, at least for the most part I was able to develop my own set of values and beliefs around money and to come to the conclusion that getting as much education as possible and earning income from a career of my choice would be the path to riches for me as an adult.

Of course, this meant that I was missing the bigger picture piece of investing, but that would come later when I became interested in owning real estate. I did own some raw land in the middle of Florida swampland, and when the developers came in and drained the swamp and began to build a company came in and decided to build a theme park. Yes, it was Disney and I was a property owner just miles away when they first planned Disney World. Also, I was only twelve years old when I purchased that land, but that is a story I will share in more detail later on.

So my goal was to do well in school and get into college with the plan of becoming a veterinarian. Because we were living in Miami during these years my mother would regularly take me to the University of Miami for various events. There were concerts and festivals, along with exhibitions and lectures. One in particular stands out in my memory involving a laser show. This was in the early 1970s when lasers were looked upon as science fiction. I equated college with this university at that time and dreamed of attending that school until I got a little older and realized there were many choices. But I will forever be grateful that my mother exposed me to the idea of going to college in this way.

I loved animals and wanted them to play a major role in my life. For two summers my best friend and I volunteered at the Crandon Park Zoo on Key Biscayne in Miami. This zoo was moved to a larger location in 1981 and then destroyed during Hurricane Andrew in August of 1992 and another was rebuilt a year later, so my memories of time spent there are even more precious to me all these years later.

We would catch a bus at six in the morning to go downtown, and then transfer to another bus to take us to Crandon Park. We began our shift at nine o'clock sharp and could not be late, as many animals were depending on us to feed them and clean their cages. The work was messy, the days were hot and humid, and the zoo's employees were not always friendly and welcoming to us, but we loved being a part of it all.

What I didn't realize at the time was the power of volunteering as a way to get experience in an area of interest to you. So even though I was a volunteer and even incurred travel expenses during these two summers when I was twelve and thirteen years old, this experience became invaluable when I applied for paid positions with veterinarians when I was sixteen and seventeen years old.

So one thing led to another and during those teenage years I developed my own beliefs and values around money, and a certain sense of financial responsibility that would carry into my adult years. This included, but was not limited to:

- Volunteering is an excellent path to being paid for work you want to do
- Trading time for money is the way it works in the real world
- Many times you will work at a job that is stressful and not joyous in any way, but you must stick with it if you want to succeed
- Furthering your education is the key to being able to earn more income for the same amount of time, and hopefully doing something you enjoy
- Starting a business is something only the wealthy or connected people are able to do
- Saving money from what you earn allows you a certain amount of freedom to do what you love from time to time
- Purchasing real estate is only for the wealthy and the rest of the population will most likely rent their place of residence forever

- Unless you win the lottery, your place in the working world cannot change until you return to school to learn a new set of skills that are in high demand

When I type this list I realize just how limited my thinking was during those years. Of course, we must all begin somewhere and then move forward if we wish to make progress in the direction we wish to pursue. Everything I listed here was based on my own experiences and the beliefs and values I incorporated into my thinking along the way. All of those years I was maneuvering the course of life without a captain.

Imagine the child in your life going through decades of adult life without the foundation that would best serve them and the people in their life. This is where you come in and the primary reason I wrote this book. Your mentoring will open up a new world for your child and allow them to reach for greater goals and to fulfill their highest potential. Yes, earning personal income is a worthy goal, but the bigger picture offers so many additional possibilities and opportunities.

Saving, Spending, Investing, and Giving

Laying the Ground Rules

Money is not intended solely for spending. If you do not discuss the topics of saving money, making investments, and giving money to others with the child in your life, you are missing a great opportunity to broaden their horizons and enlighten them beginning at an early age. And if you believe in giving allowances, whether based on completing chores, good behavior, or "just because" you may have already set up patterns that will lead to beliefs and values that are not even the ones you follow in your own financial life and wish to pass on for future generations.

Remember that the ultimate goal with all of this is financial responsibility, and this requires ongoing discussion, involvement, and evaluation to truly be effective in shaping your child's future. Demanding they drop half of their allowance into their piggy bank or savings account and spend the other half on anything they want to purchase is a concept that may have seen better days. This could be updated for modern times and more evolved thinking.

The big idea here is that you want to emulate the experiences your child will encounter in their "real life" as an adult, and in the hopes of mirroring some of what you can anticipate decades earlier give them an opportunity to navigate through a simulator of your creation. Imagine being able to practice as a child what we will face as an adult; it's possible when you set some ground rules and then adhere to them.

Saving is the best place to begin with this, in my opinion. Take a close look at what you personally have been practicing in this area over the past decade or so. Do you put aside a specific amount or a percentage of your income every month or with some schedule of regularity? How did you come to this conclusion as a way to save? Is this savings for a specific reason, such as a trip or other special occasion, is it to make sure you have six months or a year's worth of savings in case you face a financial or medical or other unforeseen emergency or hardship? Is it a specific dollar amount, or a percentage of your gross or net income?

Once you've had the chance to examine your own behavior in this area, ask yourself what you would do the same or differently if you were at your first job or just out of college today.

Now it's time to open the discussion with your child. If you already have some rules in place around this, or engage in regular conversations on this topic, announce that you wish to revisit it and have a more meaningful conversation now that they are older and more mature.

I prefer the idea of spending for what you need and want - remember our earlier conversation on this important topic of distinguishing needs from wants - and then saving whatever is left over for emergencies and unforeseen life events. But you must come to your own conclusions and be open to changing your thinking over time as new situations arise.

Investing...Even for Little Kids

In my experience I have found that children as young as about eight years old can begin to understand the concepts of investing money, defined here as the process of placing money into an entity that may or may not yield a positive return over time. Depositing money in a savings account would be a low-risk investment, whereas investing in the stock market would be significantly more risky. I am not an expert in this area by any means, so my beliefs and practices may be skewed based on my personal experiences. Earlier I told you that I had invested in a piece of raw land when I was only twelve years old. This is the story around that...

One day I saw an advertisement in a magazine about buying land in the Central Florida area. There was a little form you could tear out of the magazine and send in with your down payment and your first month's payment. It was twenty dollars down and twenty dollars a month for ten years and I thought this was the key to the magic kingdom of riches. It was for a tiny piece, about one sixth of an acre of raw land, meaning that no water or other utilities were anywhere nearby and might not be for decades. This sounded heavenly to me at that time. I sent in my postal money order and forgot to even mention it to my mother. Perhaps I was thinking I could surprise her one day with a new house where we could live that I could build on this land, but I honestly do not remember those details.

Then one day about a month later a man wearing a suit and carrying a briefcase knocked on the door. My mother answered and I heard him ask for me. She was about to tell him it was a mistake and send him away for good when I spoke up and said that he indeed had the correct house and the right person.

Over the course of the next half hour it came out that I had been the purchaser, but now that they were aware I was a minor my mother would need to hold title in her name on my behalf. The land was located in Osceola County, an up and coming area south of Orlando where developers were anxious to start building over the next decade. The year was 1967 and within another year the Disney Corporation would make an important announcement, but we knew nothing of this at that time.

At first my mother was reluctant to come aboard and agree to this arrangement, but after some dramatic pleading on my part she finally gave in. I promised to earn the twenty dollars each month and to send in the money order on time.

The rest of this story is much too long to share here, but suffice it to say that this investment was the key to the magic kingdom for my mother and I, in many respects. It opened the door to an expanded and enlightened level of thinking for each of us as to our futures, as people coming from and whom had only known great poverty in the past. And with that came a financial responsibility and commitment, even if it was only twenty dollars on the first of each month.

I still believe real estate to be a solid and wise investment, even though the climate has changed drastically over the years. You must decide if you will share your life experiences in investing in real estate, the stock market, bonds, commodities (remind me sometime to share my experience with coffee futures in the late 1970s), or something else altogether with the child in your life. As their trusted guide and mentor it is up to you to introduce this subject and move forward in a way that makes sense for everyone involved.

Later on we'll talk about how to handle losing money with investments, but for now I just want you to know that it is completely appropriate to pursue investment opportunities with your child, even while they are still very young. Investing can be fun, especially when your investment is increasing and is also a way to incorporate math and other academic subjects into your experience. The idea that one's money can increase over time without having to work for it must be taught to your child in a way that makes sense.

If you like vintage cars, use this as an example. If you have family members or friends in another country or know people involved in a specific industry or field of interest, look for relevant examples here. The basic premise to teach is that if you take the time and make the effort to research what you will invest in and also stay on top of what goes on over time, you are much more likely to earn money back or at least stay even on your investment rather than losing any money.

Helping People in Need

There is great joy and satisfaction in helping people who are in need. It's a simple process, where you share your time and resources with others yet many of us do not get involved with this aspect of life for a number of reasons. For me, it was because I honestly believed that I did not have enough time or enough money to make a difference. I would give a homeless person I encountered a few dollars or donate to the Red Cross and other groups once in awhile, but I didn't think anything I could do would be very important because it just wasn't enough money. And I certainly did not have any time to volunteer with my busy schedule. This was the story I told myself for many years, until I made the conscious decision to change my life completely in 2006 and I began to view life with a renewed perspective of hope, faith, charity, and goodwill. I will explain.

At some point in my childhood, and carrying over into my adult life I thought of people as "us" and "them." This was how I divided the people who had money from the people who would always be struggling to have enough money. I longed to become one of "them" and that's why I worked hard in school and in college and why over the years I took jobs I thought might give me a better opportunity to become one of "them."

But life doesn't work this way, and I only wish someone had enlightened me on how it really works when I was a much younger person. It certainly would have made my life much simpler and easier and shown me greater opportunities sooner. Instead, I learned over time that we can have almost anything we want in life and that we make our own opportunities by preparing every day. I began this section of the book with a quote from Lucius Annaeus Seneca circa 50 A.D. that goes like this:

Luck is where preparation meets opportunity.

We will all be that "someone in need" at some point in our lives. It may come when you are stranded on the side of the road, in the hospital fighting a serious illness, or when you have a life situation that renders you emotionally unable to face the day. So it makes sense to be in constant preparation to meet the opportunities to serve head on.

Teaching young people how to help and serve others will make their life's journey more complete. And it will also better prepare them for what is to come when you choose to reach for and exceed your highest potential on a daily basis. I wrote about this topic extensively in a previous book entitled *"Rethinking the Work Ethic: Embrace the Struggle and Exceed Your Own Potential"* and it has received critical acclaim for helping people to see their lives much differently than they had previously and includes steps for bringing about change of a transformational nature.

How does this relate to financial responsibility in kids and teaching values and beliefs around money?

Spending time with the child or children in your life allows you to get to know them well and to help shape their thinking, outlook, and actions. When people are in need, and they are every day on every corner of the world you can reach out and make their lives better, whether it is only for a moment or for a much longer period of time.

I joined Rotary, an international service organization in 2006. I had seen the little blue and gold wheel on signs when I drove through new cities and towns, but did not know what it was all about until I moved to a new city and started my online business as an entrepreneur. It was intimidating to me at first, but everyone was friendly and welcoming and soon I was involved in hands-on projects within my community.

One early project was where we were making alterations at the home of a returning veteran who would be in a wheelchair for the remainder of his life. I observed generations of families involved in figuring out what needed to be done and how to accomplish it quickly and efficiently. People I still know to this day served people they did not know but for whom they had great respect, and in the process they learned, taught, and shared their thoughts and ideas around life.

One family in particular comes to mind here. The grandfather had been in my Rotary Club for over forty years. His son had been a member for about fifteen years. Together they ran a local insurance company, and each of their wives was also involved on a daily basis. With them that day was the oldest grandson, who was about twelve years old at the time.

The adult son was tired that morning and complaining of how his back was hurting from riding his bicycle so far on the previous day. The other two did not make eye contact or address his complaints. Then the grandson grumbled about not being able to go somewhere with two of his friends that day because he had to work with dad and grandpa on this project. Again, these words fell on deaf ears as they ignored his words. I waited for the grandfather to complain or comment about something he would prefer to be doing on that day, but I guess he thought better of it and remained silent.

Then the hard work of figuring out what had to be done and how they would do it was upon them. I couldn't hear much of what they were saying but I got the idea they were going to build a ramp going from the detached garage up to the back door, making it easier for the veteran to get from his van into the house each time he came home after being out. They each shared their ideas with the other two, there were some disagreements here and there, and then it was time to determine which path they would take to accomplish their goal.

At some point I came to the conclusion this was a family who had their own internal communication and were used to problem solving as a team and family unit. By the end of the afternoon the new ramp was in place and they looked at one another with great family pride. When the veteran came rolling down the driveway he had a huge smile on his face and gratitude in his eyes. His toddler daughter was sitting in his lap and she offered a high five to the grandson, who gently answered her gesture with a tiny high five in return.

The point I wish to make here is that everyone has a place in their family and those roles will become interchangeable over time. If you apply these principles of helping those in need to communicating responsibility and family values around finances and other important issues you are bound to have greater success than people who keep to themselves and tend to be an island rather than a part of a cohesive team.

Losing Money and How to Handle It

Not all investments pay off. That's just the fact of the matter and many times this is due to circumstances beyond your control. The key to success with financial responsibility is being able to handle these occasions, minimize the net loss, and move forward with confidence and savvy you did not possess before this situation occurred.

When it comes to teaching financial responsibility and values to the child in your life this area alone can provide some of the best lessons and examples they will internalize and carry through to their own children and beyond. Honesty and openness, to the level and degree that is appropriate for the child's age and maturity will prove crucial to the process. Encourage questions that go into deeper areas and details that will bring the story to life. There is nothing that replaces life lessons based on real life.

Investing in real estate is an area that serves as relatable to everyone. We all live in real estate whether we own or rent. I highly recommend discussing this with your child as early as possible, explaining the difference between owning and renting the domicile in which you live, and your beliefs in why one model is superior and may have advantages over the other.

I was aware at an early age that my mother and I were living in apartments we rented from month to month, and that if you did not have the money to pay you would be forced to vacate the premises quickly. Then when I was twelve years old we moved into a house that was owned by out of state family members and our attitude towards real estate changed significantly. That was also the year I became a property owner when I purchased the raw land by mail order, a story I shared here earlier.

Real estate can be seen as a worthwhile investment to many people, but the big picture is far from rosy in many cases. Explain to your child that the commitment to owning the home in which you live versus that required as a renter. There are taxes to be paid, repairs and upgrades to be made, and ongoing issues with the property itself, the neighborhood, and the community that must be taken seriously when you are a homeowner. Renting or leasing a property gives you less stability, but the flexibility of being able to relocate rather quickly could be advantageous in many cases. Purchasing real estate to rent or lease out to others is also worthwhile on many levels, but the downside can take both a financial and emotional toll on the property owners and their families over time.

Remember here that beliefs and values around property ownership tend to be passed down through generations, and that someone whose family has never owned their own residence is much less likely to pursue home ownership on their own. I was enthralled by the idea of owning property, to the point that I became a licensed real estate agent while still in my early twenties, rolled that into a broker's license several years later, and then became a certified residential appraiser within two years from then. I continue to be a real estate broker in California, but have only represented myself and family members since starting my online business in 2006.

I'm not even discussing ownership of commercial, industrial, or agricultural real estate, which are investment opportunities that do not require occupancy by the owner and can be much less of a hands on undertaking.

The important thing to discuss with your child on an ongoing basis is that real estate, like any other investment is not a sure thing, and that you must consider many sides of a purchase before signing on the dotted line. I always say that we are all brilliant while the market is going up, and once the downturns hit or there are extenuating circumstances beyond our control with the economy, natural disasters, and more then we all become students once again.

I will take the opportunity here to discuss credit. It seems like once you reach age eighteen the credit card companies are lying in wait, ready to pounce on you and convince you of the power of buying what you want now and postponing payment until later. As your child's trusted financial educator and advisor, you must begin these conversations around obtaining and managing credit at least two years earlier, around the age of sixteen. My recommendation is to give provide them with a credit card from your account as early as possible, with a limit of perhaps five hundred to a thousand dollars. Then require them to sit down with you once a month to go over their spending habits and patterns, as well as the statement. A discussion of credit ratings and the importance of building and maintaining a high credit rating will ensue and you may well avoid any surprises once they are legally able to obtain credit on their own.

The stock market is another area of investing where you may lose money. Again, I am not an expert on any level with this, so I would recommend that you find and connect with people you trust and then dip your toe into the water before taking a full body plunge. I have friends who continue to come out ahead with their stock, bond, and mutual fund investments and portfolios, but I believe it is due to their steadfastness in staying on top of what is happening with these markets, many times on a daily basis.

The other investment I will mention is with a startup or other business. To my line of thinking this may be the most risky of anything I have discussed here, but it is also the most exciting and valuable in many ways. Being in on the ground floor of a business that it begun with passion and enthusiasm from people who will devote at least a part of their daily lives to creating something that will change the world is an awesome opportunity to be a part of history. Imagine being in the garage or at least in the neighborhood where Steve Jobs and Steve Wozniak first discussed ideas that would become Apple in the future.

What's Next?

Discipline is the bridge between
goals and accomplishment.
~ Jim Rohn

I have already discussed many topics related to kids and money in this book, and by now you have come to many of your own conclusions about what is best for you and for the child or children in your life. You may have even discovered that you are more opinionated than you thought before you began reading and thinking about these topics and how you've been previously handling them. The subtitle for this book is "teaching financial responsibility and values to children", so it makes sense that I would want to share more about the family connection to financial responsibility.

In these last two chapters - *It's a Family Affair* and *Beliefs and Practices at Every Stage of Life* I go into more details about the great value of community when it comes to helping shape the financial future of a young person.

It takes a village to raise and nurture and educate a child, so you will want to include not only your family members but also friends, business associates, and thought leaders in this process. Attending events in person and creating a reading this is a part of this process. Your child will encounter a plethora of people on their own once they become adults, so I believe it is best to be more selective with who they are influenced by while they are still under eighteen.

And in the interest of frugal people everywhere, I have included an Appendix on *Budgeting with Children* in which I share a plethora of tips and ideas for having fun, making ends meet, and just doing things in a more financially thoughtful way with your kids.

It is my sincere hope that this information is helpful and makes sense to you on some level and that it opens up these topics as ones for discussion at the very least.

It's a Family Affair

But Grandma Always Did It This Way!

Conversations and interactions around money and finances in general have a way of becoming a part of your family blueprint, much the way other traditions are passed down through the generations. Sometimes they lead to positive outcomes with the beliefs and values that are shared, and other times your family members may simply be doing things in a certain way because someone years ago always did it this way. I'll share a story here that makes this point well, I believe.

A young couple is newly married and the bride happily announces she is going to prepare a ham for her husband, using a family recipe handed down for generations. The husband is thrilled to hear this and watches as his wife cuts off the end of the ham before placing it gently into the oven. He is curious as to why this step is necessary and asks her to explain. She responds that her mother always cut off the end of the ham before placing it in the pan, adding some ingredients, and then baking it at the right temperature and for just the right amount of time. "This is how mom always did it," she states proudly.

The husband smiles and nods, but questions just why the cutting off of one end of the ham is a part of this family recipe and tradition. He politely excuses himself from the kitchen and calls his new mother-in-law to inquire about these details. She tells him that her mother always did it this way, but that she does not know the exact reason for this. She thinks that perhaps it has something to do with the juices from the ham being released more quickly and easily than if it were not cut on one end.

Now this new husband, an engineer I should mention is more curious than ever, so he calls up his wife's grandmother to ask her about the recipe and the cooking method. She makes him promise not to breathe a word of what she is about to tell him to anyone, and once he agrees she says, "My mother and father lived in a tiny apartment with a very small oven. The only way to get the ham to fit into the pan that would be used to bake it in the oven was to cut off one end. My mother was embarrassed by this and when she taught me to cook she told me to always cut off the end of the ham and use a smaller baking pan so that I could prepare this meal no matter where I would live over the course of my life."

It turned out that the great grandma had a reason for cutting off the end of the ham. The next three generations did not, and didn't even know why they were going through these motions each time they prepared the family recipe. Instead, they were blindly following a tradition passed down to them without rhyme or reason. It was because "Grandma always did it this way."

This may be a humorous story about the ham, but it's not so funny if you and your family are engaged in financial habits and traditions that have no rhyme or reason for what you wish to accomplish and to share with the children in your life. I would encourage you to take a close look at everything you do around earning, spending, saving, investing, giving, and other decisions large and small and decide if these actions are worth continuing as they are or if they need further review and possible change or alteration. Just as a small business or an international corporation would have quarterly reviews on all aspects of their procedures, goals, and results, you can do this as a family.

I initiated goal setting in my family almost ten years ago, and we all look forward to continuing with it every year. Typically this occurs during the week between Christmas and

New Year's and now includes family members as young as fourteen. We begin with an open discussion of where we are now, and this includes all aspects of our lives, not just the financial pieces.

As we go from person to person, everyone has the opportunity to share how they feel about the year that is about to pass and new one that will soon arrive. When we get to the discussion around money, each person shares their financial goals for the current year, what they were able to accomplish, what they wish to work on and complete for the new year, and how each of us can play a part in helping them to achieve the results and outcome they have in mind.

One of my granddaughters wanted to move from the competitive ice skating team she had been on since she was about eight years old to another team that was headed for the professional circuit. This would require hard work, and also more expensive skates and other equipment and the cost to travel to the nearly cities where this team practiced and performed.

She asked each of us to help her, and she asked me specifically to share with her on a regular basis quotes and stories about people who have achieved difficult goals. I did that all summer and in the fall she announced to us that she had been accepted on to the new team. Of course, it was her daily commitment to practice and to eat properly and stay focused that was the part of this process she needed to do on her own, but the rest of us loved being involved and included in this goal in our own small ways.

Another example I will share is when my stepdaughter decided to return to school to earn her nursing degree. She knew she was in for three full years of hard work and dedication. She had carefully written down her goals of working on two degrees simultaneously and what she needed from each of her children, her husband, and from each of the non-immediate family members to help her succeed. Money and financial responsibility was a part of this journey, but there was so much more involved here.

When she graduated recently, with honors I might add, each of us felt like we had helped her in some way. This is an excellent example of how to make every life decision a family affair and to make sure everyone is in agreement and on the same page as much as possible. Whether a family member's goal will take six weeks during the summer or three years of college or postgraduate study, making it a family affair is a very good idea, I honestly believe.

Learning *From* Your Child

At some point in time while the children in our lives are growing up, a situation arises where we realize and acknowledge that we are learning *from* our child instead of them only learning from us. It's a moment of mixed emotions for everyone, as you come to terms with the fact that your relationship with this child will be changed forevermore.

In my case, this moment came when my stepson, at eight years of age, informed me that much of what I knew about sports was incorrect and "old-fashioned" and proceeded to school me on the rules of football and basketball. I laughed, not at him but with him as he used a drawing tablet to write notes and draw crude pictures to share the information he wanted, or perhaps more accurately, needed for me to know if he and I were to continue watching college and professional basketball and football games on a regular basis. He was right, of course and I forced myself to suck it up and thank him for his honesty and straightforwardness in this matter.

That same little boy, now a man with children of his own is currently my financial advisor and a business partner on many of my ongoing projects in both business and real estate, and I believe that all began on that day when I was able to see him as more of an equal than I had at any time in the past. The way I handled the situation all those years ago set the stage for him to have the confidence in his own ideas and abilities to be able to speak frankly and to take a stand on his beliefs.

And he has now passed this line of thinking down to his own children, my grandchildren in a way that makes me proud on a daily basis. I am in awe of the way they interact, and in the confidence and pride they exhibit when they come up with thoughts and ideas they wish to explore further. Every new idea is greeted with wonder and possibility, even though most do not make it to fruition because of the fatal flaws that are exposed as the discussion gets more detailed. But some of these ideas that were left for dead have since been resurrected as the technology caught up with them or for a plethora of others reasons. How I wish I had been raised in this way!

What can kids teach you? Plenty, it turns out, if you take the time to explore this further. As a classroom teacher I was anxious to learn from my students. Even at ten or eleven years of age they had experienced more than I had in many areas of their lives. Most of them had either immigrated to the United States at a much younger age, or been born here to parents who did not speak or understand a word of English. Those two factors alone gave them unique insight into the world around them and the ability to adapt and assimilate into a culture that was quite different than what they had been born into and required them to learn a new set of rules in order to succeed.

Over my twenty years of teaching this described children who hailed from Eastern Europe after the dissolution of the Soviet Union at the end of 1991, coming from countries now known as Latvia, Armenia, Estonia, Uzbekistan, and Russia. I also taught kids from the Central American countries of Nicaragua, Guatemala, Mexico, and El Salvador. In addition, I had students in my classrooms during these years from

Vietnam, many of whom had parents who escaped during the refugee program as "boat people" during the 1970s after the Vietnam War ended in 1975 and into the 1980s.

How does this relate to money? You may be asking. I believe that people of all ages and from a wide variety of backgrounds and cultures possess incredibly valuable ideas to share with others. By starting with this precept we empower the kids in our life to begin nurturing their unique and innovative ideas and with having the courage to let them be known without the fear of being ridiculed or ignored. The best way to build upon this is to engage in serious conversations about money and financial responsibility with as many members of the family as possible on a regular basis, and I recommend it be at least once each month. Make it a family meeting and this can be done in person if possible and virtually, if necessary.

This can be an excellent time to bring other generations into the mix when it comes to discussing this sometimes sensitive and controversial topic. Being able to have representatives from two or more generations at the table ensures that your conversations will be lively, educational, and insightful from more than one perspective. In a world where ageism is prevalent and people's ideas tend to be valued less over time, it can be refreshing to value knowledge and experience that has been aged as fine wine might be in a different setting.

Generational Values Through the Ages

Something very interesting has happened in the past decade or two, or at least that is when I first became aware of this. It's the phenomenon of multi-generation families, where people from four different generations either live in the same household, or in two households within a twenty or thirty minute drive of each other. What is different is that we now have five different generations involved, whereas in the past it was typically limited to three. The primary reason for this is that people are living longer, healthier lives and also generations are a few years shorter right now than they have averaged over the past fifty years or so.

When it comes to kids and money this can be an excellent scenario in order to teach and learn about finance from five different perspectives. It also opens up the opportunity to create a legacy of financial values and beliefs within your own bloodline and descendancy. This legacy can serve as a storytelling device to speak your truth to those who are a part of your family and to compare and contrast the similarities and differences from one generation to another. What you think and believe today is in pert a reflection of what your ancestors believed, but in a modern format. I recommend that you dive into this process as soon as possible to include as many points of view as are available at the present time.

The five generations I'm including here are:
1) Silent/Greatest Generation - born circa 1917-1945
2) Baby Boomers - born circa 1946-1964
3) Generation X - born circa 1965-1980
4) Generation Y or "Millennials" - born circa 1981-1995
5) Generation Z - born circa 1996 to the present day

There will always be differences in beliefs between the generations, and those around money may tend to be more controversial than ones about most other things. With five generations currently alive on our planet, we have the opportunity to learn from and have open discussions around the topics of financial responsibility, spending habits, and finances in general from people both older and younger than ourselves. This is a unique time in our history that must not be overlooked or taken for granted.

It also makes perfect sense that people of different ages would think and act in unique ways when it comes to money.

We have all had years of experiences and time to form our own beliefs and values based on what we have gone through and the conclusions we have come to, on our own and with the help of parents, mentors, employers, friends, and more.

In an effort not to make too many generalizations about any single age group, let's think about how people react to financial and other situations in their everyday life based on their prior and ongoing experiences. Then we can draw some conclusions about how we can choose to learn from other people's experiences while forming our own belief system and values.

If you have gone through great financial hardship in your life, whether as a child or during adulthood this will affect how you think about money, your spending and saving habits, and your future financial decisions. This would be people who came of age and lived through the Great Depression during the 1930s or one of the economic recessions that have occurred every twenty years or so since the 1950s or the Great Recession, which means everyone who is alive today. The Great Recession was related to the financial crisis of 2007–08 and U.S. mortgage crisis of 2007–09. This approximately nineteen month period resulted in the collapse of much of the financial sector in the world economy. This set into motion a decline in our trust in real estate and stocks as an investment and at the eleventh hour the banks were bailed out by the U.S. government. The Great Recession was experienced differently around the world, with North America and Europe fully involved and more newly developed economies like China and India growing substantially during this time.

Also included here are people who were willing to be more risky with investments in the stock market or real estate over their lifetimes, or those whose businesses went under as a result of being forced out of the marketplace when trends changed and they did not keep up with these changes.

If money has never been an obstacle for you because your family put things in place, perhaps before you were born, your view of money will be a unique one and not shared by very many others in the world. This refers to people who were set up with trust funds or inherited money without having to do anything to receive it. This group tends to know very little about managing finances and is often dependent upon others to advise them.

If you somehow created wealth as a young adult or older based on something you did that were perceived as being of great value to others, your view of money will also be unique. This would include people in the arts, athletes, those who created companies that did very well, and others who in some way contributed to the world and were able to monetize it over time. You may believe that money is simply the byproduct of serving others and sharing your talents and abilities and that financial wealth can be easily created over and over again.

People of the Silent/Greatest generation and era tend to be more conservative than the norm, are compulsive savers, maintain a low income to debt ratio and use more secure financial products like CDs (Certificates of Deposit) as compared to stocks. They also tend to feel a responsibility to leave a legacy to their children, are extremely patriotic, and are oriented to put work before pleasure. This generation begins with people born in 1917, so let's take a closer look at what was happening during that year.

In 1917 the United States formally entered World War I. Woodrow Wilson is at the beginning of his second term as the 28th President. Women win the right to vote in New York State; it would be three more years before the Nineteenth

Amendment to the United States Constitution would give all women the right to vote.

People of the baby Boomer generation, beginning in 1946 had significantly more job and higher education opportunities as World War II ended and an economic boom took over America. Those born during this era tend to value security and comfort for themselves and their families.

Let's take a closer look at a year during this period.

In 1955 Rosa Parks refuses to obey bus driver James F. Blake's order that she give up her seat to make room for a white passenger in Montgomery, Alabama and is arrested, leading to the Montgomery Bus Boycott. The first nuclear-generated electrical power is sold commercially. The Pentagon announces a plan to develop intercontinental ballistic missiles (ICBMs) armed with nuclear weapons. President Dwight D. Eisenhower sends the first U.S. advisors to South Vietnam, beginning an almost twenty year conflict that divided the United States and changed the way we thought of military service and government action.

Generation X is what people born starting in 1965 are commonly referred to in this categorizing of modern times and generations. This was the first generation of "latchkey" kids, as divorce rates increased along with daycare. Apathy with politics and the economy is at an all time high during this time and the phrase "lost generation" is applied to those who become inactive and withdrawn. This is also the "me" generation where everyone who participates received a trophy, regardless of performance and higher education once again becomes a top priority in the United States. People are less likely to marry and start a family at an early age.

Let's take a closer look at a year during this period.

In 1968 then President Lyndon B. Johnson signed a bill eliminating the "gold cover" (the reserve backing by gold) for Federal Reserve notes and Congress repeals the requirement for a gold reserve to back U.S. currency, thus taking the United States off the gold standard. The war in Vietnam is at maximum occupation of troops and with more and more people doubting that this war can be won. Civil unrest leads to increased civil rights demonstrations. The Reverend Martin Luther King, Jr. and U.S. Senator Robert Kennedy are assassinated. Trust in government and policies begin to decline.

Generation Y, also referred to as the Echo Boomers (most are the offspring of Baby Boomers) or Millennials are technologically savvy, having been born circa 1981 and into a time where computers were on the horizon and increasing their power daily. They tend to be precocious without apology, more in tune with and accepting of diversity, and are ready to spend money on creature comforts and luxury items. They are fearless when it comes to pursuing opportunities and dreams for unprecedented lifestyle design. Generation Y is confident, assertive, and supportive of people and causes worldwide in a way that is unparalleled in recorded history. Their opinions have been included in financial transactions since they were very young and they are capable of making decisions that are beyond their years when it comes to finance in general.

Let's take a closer look at a year during this period.

In 1989 the first commercial internet service providers open their virtual doors. F. W. de Klerk is elected in South Africa, gradually dismantling the apartheid system over the next five years, culminating with the 1994 election that brings ANC (African National Congress) leader Nelson Mandela to power. Genetic modification of adult human beings is tried for the first time in a gene tagging trial. Tiananmen Square protests of 1989 result in hundreds being killed with automatic rifles and tanks.

Generation Z is the generation that began joining the planet circa 1996 and may surprise us most of all. The future is always anticipated with a mixture of excitement and trepidation and this newest generation will be no different.

While we don't know much about Gen Z yet we do know much about the culture and environment they are growing up in right now. Diversity is a basic and crucial piece of who they are and many appear to be color blind on a level the rest of us cannot fully fathom. What we do comprehend is that higher levels of technology will change the face of education and allow for more customized, multi-media rich instruction and accelerated learning and achievement opportunities in a previously unprecedented manner.

I won't choose a year to examine as representative of this group because history is being written on a moment by moment basis and unfolding in new and exciting ways for those of us watching.

There is true generational value through the ages when it comes to teaching and learning financial responsibility and values. Make every effort to take full advantage of having ready access to the experience, thoughts, and opinions of so many generations at one time, and perhaps under your roof. Even though there will be wide discrepancies when it comes to beliefs and value systems, we can all only benefit from what is shared when we choose to have open and honest conversations around teaching financial responsibility and values to the child in our life.

Beliefs and Practices at Every Stage of Life

Teaching Kids to Make Their Own Financial Decisions

One of the goals of parenting is to raise strong, independent children who are both willing and capable of carrying on their lives in a way that serves them as the unique individuals they are. Much of the time this works out, while at other times there is a breakdown in the process and everything begins to slowly unwind and fall apart.

You know your own child or the child in your life better than most of the people they are spending time with do, because you are focused on their success and well-being. When we know someone well we are able to provide a set of lessons and examples that will serve them along their own journey and guide them to becoming the financially responsible adults we know they can be. The goal is to do this in such a way as to allow them to learn from their own mistakes and come to their own conclusions. It's a part of critical thinking that must be followed so that each human being can think for themselves and reach their full and highest potential.

In teaching kids to make their own financial decisions, and ones that will serve them well over a lifetime we will provide opportunities for success through ongoing experiences. A crucial piece of this is to allow a misstep along the way, as this is the way the brain's synapses make the connections that lead to clearer, more focused thinking that is logical as well and perhaps more empathetic. I am not an expert in the area of brain science but continue to study this incredible part of our physiology and the results that are not only possible, but probable under the most optimal of circumstances.

This can begin at a very early age. Does your child prefer a scoop of vanilla or chocolate ice cream? I am constantly around parents who have concluded that you cannot ask a child to choose from among more than two choices. To this I say why not? If we limit the world of possibility from the earliest moments of cognition aren't we stifling the decision making process within their minds from that moment forward? The world is so much more than vanilla or chocolate. Perhaps they will choose strawberry, or butter pecan, or another type of dessert altogether or no dessert at all. And just maybe the ability to say no to peer pressure begins with being able to think through your choices and instead of choosing between two things the child is now able to speak up and make a different choice or to just say "no" to all choices available on that day. Something to think about and food for thought, that's for sure.

As you weave your way through the common beliefs that are put forward by parents, teachers, and experts in this area of money and kids, remember that you are the one laying the foundation and setting the ground rules. Perhaps this was one reason I was drawn to this topic and am writing this book; financial education, values, and responsibility is a very personal part of our lives and we must come to our own conclusions. You will notice that I have not used the word "should" at any place in this writing and that I am simply sharing a variety of methods and strategies that you may choose to incorporate into your own situation.

Back to helping your child to make their own financial decisions now. The brain is an organ that requires ongoing stimulation and input in order to serve us well. Give it too much time off or deny it the proper nutrients and it will slowly pull back. From what I have studied the worse things you can do to your brain include feeding it too little protein and not asking it to problem solve on a daily basis. And just as we want the child in our life to be physically fit, we must also have the goal of mental fitness at every turn. How is this best achieved? In my opinion, it is through ongoing lessons and examples along with a dialogue that is Socratic in nature.

Every day brings new opportunities for this, and they need not be age or topic appropriate in order to achieve the desired results. Bring your child into the conversations of life early on and get their brain working. When muscles ache and brains sweat you know you are moving in the right direction.

Financial Stress and Children

The kids in your life are stressed out, and financial stress is a big part of this. In fact, the topic of financial stress and your children is growing year by year.

When you have stress around money and finances, the children in your life pick up on it. Whether they are three years old or seventeen, they know when money is an issue at home. If you avoid the issue or refuse to discuss it with them, what they will imagine will be far worse than the truth of the situation. So it's best to get the conversation started and use the financial issues at home become teaching moments over time.

Your kids will react in a variety of ways when they pick up on their parents' financial problems, and here are some ways to handle these situations when it hits home.

Children will sometimes withdraw, avoiding friends and social situations. Encourage them to spend time with the people and activities they enjoy. And make sure they know that some information is private for the family only, and not to be shared with even close friends.

Young people are more attuned to situations than you might believe. Schedule a time with your spouse to sit down with your children for an open and honest discussion. Assure them that they are your first priority and that you are doing what is necessary to get back on track financially.

Many kids will react to financial stress by acting out and engaging in risky behavior. Make it clear that this is not acceptable and will not be tolerated and that you are there for them now and always. Tell them you love them, as this practice ends many times as children get older.

Feelings of helplessness may occur in older children. They feel like they would like to help with the family's financial problems but are unsure how to do this. Discuss some age appropriate options for them to be included in what is going on at home right now. Younger children, defined as those ten and under, need to be reassured that their basic needs of food and shelter are not in jeopardy and that everything will return to normal over time.

Pre-teens and young teens, ages eleven to fourteen need to know some of the details of what is going on, and to observe for themselves that you are confident in your ability to get the family's financial health back on track as soon as possible.

Older teens and young adults still living at home are best involved in the solution, to the degree and extent you and your spouse fell comfortable in sharing this part of your life with them. Discussing ways to save money and to cut back on expenses may be appropriate, such as eliminating premium channels from your cable service and choosing a less costly family vacation. This is an excellent lesson in financial responsibility, as they can see firsthand how you can do things differently to save money and still have an excellent, enjoyable experience.

And explaining to all of the kids in your life about the relationship between the cost of an item and the number of hours or amount of work that must be done in order to pay for it becomes imprinted on the brain for a lifetime. Be careful with teaching and explaining this concept however, or you may find that you have helped to create children who become too frugal and aware of spending money to enjoy life as adults. I have a grandson who refused to spend a penny of his savings when he was six and seven years old. We finally had a serious discussion with him and now he joyfully spends about a quarter to a third of what he has saved once a month. He now has a more healthy attitude toward money, and we are sure his future wife and children will appreciate our efforts.

And those feelings of helplessness can also cause havoc with your child's and your own health. Stress you carry for a long period of time can be detrimental to your health, causing problems with the immune system, energy levels, and can even cause an increased risk for cancer and heart disease. It's critical that you handle stress in an appropriate way so that your money stress won't turn into a life changing illness for you or another family member. Financial stress and your children is now a topic among pediatricians, psychiatrists, and other health care professionals.

Plan weekly outings with your children to fight off physical fatigue and keep everyone's immune system healthy. You may live where you are close by parks and trails that can be accessed all year long, or at least not too far away from where you are. These times together could be the catalyst for change within your family as you work through issues together. Remember that your financial problems don't have to be permanent.

Financial Responsibility for Couples

At some point your child will become one half of a couple. And even though you have raised this child to think for themselves and to make wise choices and decisions regarding finances, you may find yourself questioning what transpires within their relationship with another person on a regular basis.

This is because your child only represents half of this relationship and their significant other has also been raised with a set of values and beliefs based on what they took away from their parents while they were growing up. Throw into the mix what friends, other adult family members, and adult role models had to say and your voice becomes smaller and smaller over time.

I recommend that you sit down with the couple at the earliest moment and begin a dialog around the topic of financial responsibility. Try to find out how they were raised and what experiences may have impacted them in this area. Make a plan to meet the parents, whether or not they have already become in laws through marriage. Waiting until then may not give you the time to share your thoughts on their current actions and future plans.

This can all begin when your child begins to date. Even though there is little chance this will be the person they will ultimately settle down with years later, this is excellent practice for you to get used to how it will be in the future. Decisions about where to go on a date, how much to spend on dinner and a movie, and what to focus on with school and jobs is the beginning of lifelong decisions that must be made. While your child is still a minor you have more say so as to what they do, and this experience will benefit everyone involved. Here is an example from my own life...

When I heard from family friend Gary after an absence of several years he was almost thirty years old and had been living with Julia for three years. She wanted to purchase a home with Gary before they got married so they could live somewhere that was an investment rather than a rental property. Gary was reluctant to take this step for several reasons. He felt that people should be married before they purchased property together and he believed that once they took this step Julia would insist on them having a child together. Julia interpreted Gary's feelings as ones of doubt about their future as a couple. This issue was tearing them apart and taking them further away from each other and the life they both so wanted to share.

It turned out that Gary had spent almost no time with Julia's family over the years they had been dating and then moved in together. Julia had come to know Gary's family quite well during this time and had become close with them. When they came to me as a long time friend of Gary and his family I suggested that both families begin getting together regularly and begin the process of open and honest discussions around family, money, marriage, and children.

When I heard from them the next time, almost six months later Gary and Julia were engaged to be married the following spring. They had purchased a home together as an investment but continued to live in the home they had been renting. Gary shared that he had become close to Julia's father and one of her brothers and they had gone fishing and camping twice so far. Julia continued to enjoy time spent with Gary's family and was happy that both families were merging in a natural way.

Situations do not always turn out as well as this one, so make the commitment to be a positive force in the life of your child after they become one half of a couple. This is the mature way to deal with your child as they get older and will also help you to better understand the perspective of someone you don't know and may not like as a person who may come to have great influence over the child you have known and been a part of the life of since their birth.

In my own family there were two people who had gone through an unhappy divorce decades earlier and refused to speak to one another for any reason. As their child got older and finally married I stepped in to negotiate with both of them. I reminded them that one day there would be a grandchild they would both want to spend time with and that perhaps it was time for the two of them to make amends and move forward in a more unified way. This reunification took several years to get off the ground and today there are three grandchildren who are thrilled to have these grandparents a part of their lives. The decades have softened each of their hearts and everyone benefits in the process. They would both agree that their reunification of sorts was valuable for everyone involved, including each of them.

Learning From Experiences

There is no greater teacher than experience. With that said, let's explore some experiences that you may wish to present to the child in your life over time. The idea is to decide what to include in a more formal way and what to leave to chance in a more spontaneous way. There is a distinct difference with each approach and one style may be more suitable over the other at specific times during your child's life.

Let's explore five areas where experiential learning will be advantageous. These would be:

- Earning
- Saving
- Spending
- Investing
- Giving

When you are a child, earning comes in two forms. These would be by receiving an allowance and from doing some type of work in exchange for money.

Saving may be adding money to a piggy bank or other location at home for safekeeping, or depositing money into a savings account at the bank.

Spending would include money used for items and experiences of the child's choice.

Investing is a bit trickier, but for simplicity's sake let's say you have set up a brokerage account for your child where stocks, bonds, and other financial instruments will be invested and traded in over time.

Giving would include donating to a charity or non-profit organization, tithing to a church or other religious group, or informally giving money or items to people in need.

Now let's break each of these down further to examine the opportunities for teaching and learning experiences.

If you have decided to provide a weekly allowance, you and your spouse or partner may wish to make a big deal out of first introducing the idea and the ground rules to your child. If they are the oldest or an only child this may be their first experience with this concept. It will more meaningful if you add some drama to this momentous occasion and you may want to invite grandparents and other relatives as well as close friends.

Beforehand you would have explained to your child what an allowance is, what activities or behaviors are expected in return for this money, how much it will be, the frequency of receiving it, and what it can or must be used for. This is all subject to negotiation, as you will learn as your child gets older. While I was growing up it was typical for my friends to receive their allowances from their fathers on Friday, after these dads were paid at work, cashed their checks, and arrived at home.

This is all up to you, of course. I'm putting my personal feelings aside here on this topic, as I do not believe in or adhere to the custom of giving children money as an allowance, as I shared earlier. But the majority of families do use allowance as a method of teaching children about money, so these are my ideas on how to incorporate it into your plan.

Saving money can be explained to your child as the way to be better prepared for the future and also how to be able to make a larger purchase that requires more money than you have at one time. An example within your family might include saving for a family vacation, a new car, or a down payment on a house.

Spending money is the most fun part of the process for many people, old and young alike so you'll want to provide examples of what we all spend money on in our lives. Whether it be for new school clothes, a bicycle, or just shuffling off cash while out and about spending is a part of the financial process that requires responsible thinking and actions.

Investing money can also be an exciting proposition, given that you have the possibility of multiplying the money you earn many times over. It can also mean financial loss, as I discussed in an earlier chapter. Either way, investment opportunities empower your child in a way few other experiences will be able to do during their lifetime.

Giving allows you child to become a part of the bigger picture at an early age. Children tend to internalize their feelings here and you will get to know them so much better by observing their simple acts of choosing to share what they have with other human beings. Whether your child is one that shares toys openly or clutches them tightly to their chest when someone else wants to see or touch them, teaching them about giving to people in need will help to change their perspective over time.

What would these experiences look like if you were to offer them up as scheduled lessons and teachable moments, while also taking into account the spontaneous events that occur within a lifetime? Let's take a closer look.

Receiving allowance may look like what I shared above, but add to it the child sitting on the sofa on a Friday afternoon, watching the evening news, checking the clock every two minutes, sighing audibly as the time gets later, and postponing a chore or other obligation in order to greet dad when he comes through the door after work. This is the question to ask - How did it feel when he handed you your allowance?

Now let's approach this from your child's perspective and point of view, and offer this and similar questions to solidify the experience and memory.

Saving may look like riding your bike to the bank on a chilly Saturday morning and waiting in line for your favorite teller so you may deposit ten dollars into your savings account. What did the teller say to you as you presented your cash? What other sounds could you hear while you were in the bank?

Giving may look like volunteering at the local homeless shelter and serving meals that you helped pay for. What did you see when you began giving out the food? What did someone say to you? Describe the look in someone's eyes when they met yours and thanked you for the food. How did you feel while you were there, and then right after you left the shelter?

Remember that none of us remembers the day our thinking and life changed as a result of reading a chapter in a book, but we all remember what we saw, heard, touched, and felt as a result of a specific action that took place. Offer concepts around financial responsibility and values to the child in your life experientially and know that you are making lasting memories that will be time tested and adjusted for eternity.

Conclusion

Financial responsibility is one of the most important concepts you will ever teach to a child and what you say and do now will impact their entire life in multiple and untold ways in the future. If you can imagine that something you do as an unconscious habit right now in this area may be something your great grandparents came up with more than a century ago, you can begin to understand the enormity of the impact of this subject matter.

Finances are also quite sophisticated and complex and will change and shift from generation to generation, even though the basic building blocks of values, beliefs, and practices around money will remain unchanged.

I hope this book has been helpful in guiding you to understand the role you will play in your child's life when it comes to earning, spending, saving, investing, and giving. My primary goal with sharing these concepts, methods, and strategies I have developed over the past three decades is to allow you to expand your thinking and actions as you interact with your family members of all ages and then specifically with the child or children in your life.

I wrote to you as the individual reader here, but I am aware that many families are led by a couple and that the two of you must be on the same page when it comes to financial education and sharing your beliefs and values around financial responsibility. If you find that you and your spouse, partner, or other co-parenting adult are far apart in your thinking here, use this book as a resource and a guide to bring you closer together over time.

Children raised in a home where discussions are rare and actions regularly speak louder than words may find themselves lost in a sea of ideas, beliefs, and values and prefer to base their own actions on what they have observed from another adult role model. This can be a positive experience for your child in many cases as it was for me, but I am sure you would much prefer to be a part of this area of your child's life and future if given the choice. And instead of letting the chips fall where they may, taking an active role will empower your family as a whole to seek out additional people and resources as you continue along this path and journey.

Take it one day and one step at a time, map out the strategy that feels right for you and your family right now, and then vow to stay cognizant of the pieces of the puzzle you are still exploring and vigilant in your quest for knowledge and experiences that will help you to achieve your goals. Do not depend on schools or other people or groups to provide financial education to your children.

I am honored to be on this journey with you and hope that you will reach out to me with any questions you may have and to share any personal experiences that could be helpful to others.

Appendix: Budgeting With Children

An important part of teaching financial responsibility and values begins with choices you make at home every day. You may not remember when you were first introduced to the concept of staying on a budget. For many people this is a helpful way for them to live within their means and to stay on track financially. For others, it feels like limitation and control they would prefer to avoid. Either way, staying on a budget when you have children may be the way you are able to live a lifestyle that gives you more time with your kids and peace of mind when it comes to having enough money for everything you wish to do.

Budgeting When Buying Food

Perhaps money a little tight right now and your dollars not stretching as far as they used to. In today's society it is very common to have difficulty earning enough money for the things you need most. But, knowing some basic strategies and using a few simple tricks, you can save money on the things you need to buy, like food, and learn some important things along the way. A great life skill to teach your kids is how to save money. The things you teach them about money will stay with them for life, so it's important to teach them all that you can at an age and maturity appropriate level.

Teaching the value of saving money all starts at a young age. In the process of teaching your kids to save money, teach them the value of coupons and how coupons can help you to save money. Couponing is one of the first things kids can learn because it's so easy and is the foundation for all the other money-saving tips down the road.

Here are some ways to get your kids involved in the use of coupons.

- Clip coupons for the things you buy, but only for the items you will actually use. Try shopping at stores that double or even triple the value of the coupon. Buy one get one free can be a great savings, but only if you're going to use both items before they expire. The use of coupons helps to save money in big and fast ways. Digital coupons make this faster and easier than ever before.

- Join a coupon swapping group. This type of group tends to swap items for coupons. So for example, if you have a coupon for peanut butter but you don't need peanut butter, you can go to this group and trade someone for milk, or an object you may need.

- Create a list for the grocery store and stick to it. Many people tend to go over budget because they see things at the store that they think they need when in actuality, it's not needed. By having a list, it helps you to stay focused and aware of the things you need to buy and the things that you don't.

- Do not buy items you don't need just because it's a great deal. Only buy what you know you are going to use. I said this above but it bears repeating.

- Stick to your budget - Record your monthly spending on food and look for ways to save based on your actual numbers. This will force you to become more creative with your recipes and eat healthier, more nutritious meals.

- Compare prices of different brand foods based on their weight. Bring a calculator with you or use the one on your smart phone to ensure your calculations are correct in figuring out which brand is the cheapest and most affordable.

- Buy your food in bulk. Many times, buying things in higher quantities means more money saved. Buy durable things in bulk that you'll need in the future, like paper towels, toilet paper, canned food, and beans.

- Shop for baked goods during the daytime. If you're craving something from a bakery, go during the day. This is when the bakers will be marking down all of their day-old and less popular food items. I always joke that by the time I eat my bakery items they're at least a day old anyway.

- Buy store brand items. In many cases, store brand foods are a lot cheaper than those more well-known brands. You will have some items that you prefer the name brand, but give this a try and see which ones you and your family do not notice a difference.

- Avoid processed foods as much as possible. These foods are usually more expensive, and oftentimes are much less nutritious. Buy the inexpensive but healthy items, like real (not instant or processed) oatmeal and rice that requires time (more than two minutes!) to cook.

- Plan out your weekly meals before you go shopping. This will help you to shop for only the ingredients you need for the dinners you are serving.

- Let your child help you cut the coupons out of the daily newspaper. With each new coupon you and your child cuts, explain to them what that specific coupon does and how much it saves you.

- Make your grocery list and allow your child to find any coupons that correspond to the items on the list. If they are old enough to handle scissors, allow them to cut the coupons out for you.

- If you are in a comfortable financial state where this doesn't impact you too much, tell your child that all the money saved is theirs. This won't save you money, but your child will be so excited about getting money that they'll be encouraged to save as much as possible.

- Take all of the coupons to the store with you. Then, with each new purchase and addition to your cart, allow your child to find the corresponding coupon to the item.

- Show your older kids your method for how you organize your coupons. Once they see how effective this can be, they may come to realize just how valuable coupons are in saving you money.

- Make it a family game. Have some already precut coupons available for your kids to use. Then, allow them to go into the pantry and find the items that could correspond to the coupons they have in their possession. Whoever gets the most matches of coupon to item, wins!

- When your items are placed on the conveyor belt to be scanned and checked out, allow your child to hand the cashier the coupons. This will teach them that the use of coupons should be part of your shopping routine all the time. What we do regularly becomes a part of our habits that stick.

- Have a savings jar. This type of savings jar should be put somewhere everyone can see it. With this tip, you will need to remember to write down the total amount of money you saved per visit and then put that money in the jar. This will help to show your kids just how much money that the use of coupons can save you.

Knowing how to properly shop for food is key in saving money for those other things you need. Ensure that if you are having money issues, you make some attempt to save as much money as you can wherever possible. And one last tip; eat a little something before you go food shopping so you will be less likely to make choices based on your hunger level.

Borrowing Instead of Buying as a Budget Strategy

So many people decide to buy things when they can simply borrow the same thing for less. If you borrow the item, you are saving yourself so much money and space in your home for things that you actually need to own. Listed below are some things that many people buy, but which would be more beneficial to them if they were to just borrow it.

- Books - Many people only read a book once, so why would you buy the book if you can borrow it for free or for a small fee? There is likely at least one public library located near you. If you are looking for a specific book, your library is highly likely to have it. And if one library doesn't have it, another one will.

- DVDs and movies - Like books, most people only want to watch a movie once, unless it's their favorite movie. Instead of buying a movie that you will probably only watch once, borrow it from a friend. You can even look into getting a service like Amazon Prime or Netflix because they have thousands of movies you can watch whenever you please by streaming them online.

- Tools - Before you purchase a tool, see if you can borrow or rent it. Most tools take up a lot of space and cost a decent amount of money, so borrowing the tool from a friend may be the way to go. Another option includes renting from local tool shops. Tool shops don't charge very much for a renting fee, compared to the cost of buying it outright.

- Suitcases - Traveling costs a lot of money as it is. You don't need that added cost of buying suitcases. If you travel frequently, you may want to invest in a suitcase. However, most people only travel once a year at most. In these instances, instead of going out and spending hundreds on a bag, check with your friends and relatives to see if they have one they'd be willing to let you borrow. I've done this with my family in Europe for a decade now. We share suitcases and trade them back and forth on subsequent visits.

- Sporting equipment - If you are just starting out with a sport, you may not be quite good at it yet or sure you'll fully enjoy it. Until you find those answers, check with friends and relatives to see if they have any used sports equipment you can borrow. Especially if you have young children, you know that many times they lose interest quickly. You do not want to get stuck with equipment for a sport no one is involved in any longer.

Simply put, there are other options out there for you rather than buying an item that will only take up space and you may only use once. Be wise with your money and how you spend it. If you feel as though you need to buy an item rather than borrow, do that. But first, think about whether or not you will use that item again. Also, think about what exactly you need it for. Most times, you won't need the thing you're thinking of buying more than once. I sure wish I had done this years sooner myself.

Homemade Piggy Banks

Nowadays, money is usually accessed by way of your bank account and use of a plastic card. But piggy banks are an awesome tool in helping to teach your child about the value and management of money. Instead of going out and buying a generic piggy bank, try making your own. This is a fun craft that you and your child can take part in together. Here are some different homemade piggy bank ideas for you to try.

Spend, Save, Give Piggy Bank

For this DIY piggy bank, all you will need is three Mason jars, some wood, a saw to cut three circles in the wood, and some tags to write on.

First, cut the three holes into the wood. You'll want the holes to be the same size as the opening of the Mason jar. Ensure that you (the parent) cut the holes. You can paint the wood to your child's desired color if preferred.

Then, once the holes are cut, you and your child can slip the three Mason jar openings into the hole.

The third step is to label the three Mason jars with the words Spend, Save, and Give.

This type of a piggy bank will help keep your child organized, focused, and aware of how to manage their money.

Eco-Friendly Piggy Bank

For this do-it-yourself project you will need an empty plastic bottle, a knife to cut the opening in the top, and some things to decorate with.

First, take the empty plastic bottle and cut a slit on the side big enough to fit all coins and dollar bills through. Be sure that you (the adult) is the one to do this.

Then, let your child decorate it the way they want with the arts and crafts material. They can make the bottle into a pig, or simply do as they please with it.

This super-easy piggy bank is meant for your child to see their money grow with each new "deposit" and learn how valuable money is. The piggy bank also teaches your child how to be eco-friendly and to reuse any materials available.

"Feed Daily" Piggy Bank

For this DIY, you'll need an old piggy bank you may have lying around and some paint.

Take the old piggy bank that you have and paint over it to give it a new appearance. Then, in different color paint, write on the piggy bank (once dry), "Feed Daily." This will encourage your child to "feed" the bank often and get them to understand the importance of saving as much money as they can.

Piggy banks are a great place for little ones to keep all their money. It provides them with a place to keep their money organized and well managed. Making your very own piggy bank also provides your child with a sense of creativity and eco-friendliness. It's important to teach children these key lessons. When making your own piggy bank, it's like you are killing two birds with one stone.

Budget Gifts to Make with Your Children

Doing things together with your children is the perfect way to be close to them and get to know them better as individuals. A great way to do this is by doing some arts and crafts with them and making gifts for other people. Listed below are some gift ideas that you and your child can make together - either when you're bored and looking for something to do, or have a special occasion or holiday coming up.

Hand and Footprint Apron

For this craft, all you'll need is non-toxic paint and a white apron.

First, lay the apron flat on a clean surface. Have the variety of paint colors nearby. Then, take turns dipping your child's feet and hands into the paint. Press them against the apron until the hand and foot prints are clearly shown.

Use the paint to then label each hand and foot with the child's name if you have multiple children taking part in the project. Allow the apron to dry completely before giving the apron to someone as a gift.

This gift is very thoughtful and will leave mom, grandma, or auntie feeling very loved. Every time they go to use the apron, they will think of the person who made it!

Personalized Coffee Mugs

For this craft, you will need a white mug, non-washable paints, and paint brushes.

If you are doing this project with a very young child, help them to hold the mug to prevent it from breaking. Allow your child to dip the brush into the paint and brush it onto the mug to make whatever design they may please.

This gift will leave the recipient feeling very loved and will give them a smile every time they use go to drink their coffee in the morning.

Rustic Twig Picture Frame

For this DIY, you will need hot glue, twigs, and a picture frame.

Help your child collect the twigs from outside. Ensure that there aren't any bugs or moss on the sticks. Once you've collected the twigs, you can start hot gluing them to the picture frame. Depending on how old your child is, determine whether or not they can help you use a hot glue gun or if they should just observe.

Once the twigs are surrounding the outer corners of the picture frame, set the picture frame aside to dry. Once you feel the picture frame is dry enough, you can place a picture in. This gift will give an autumnal and rustic feeling in the home.

Spending quality time with your kids making presents for people who deserve it will make you, your kids, and the recipients feel amazing. Giving is better than receiving, which is a great lesson to teach your kids while making these gifts. Another benefit is that making presents is usually a lot more inexpensive than buying them, so it's a win-win situation all the way around.

Age Appropriate Money Lessons

Even though I covered this within the book, I wanted to share a few more ideas with you here. Many people make it into their adult years not knowing how to manage their money. Too many people have gone into debt after college because of the inability to use their money in the proper way. It's crucial to learn about money at a young age with your parents and other adult role models. How you teach kids about money depends on how old they are and their level of experience and maturity. Listed below are different ways to teach your child about money based on their age.

Elementary School Level
- Use a clear jar as a piggy bank. When your child can clearly see the amount of money that they have, they can see daily how much their money grows. For example, one day, they may have one dollar. Then the next day, they might have a dollar and a dime. Make sure your make a big deal out of this. Seeing how much money they have, and knowing how much the money is worth, is important in showing them how convenient it is to have their own money.
- Show them the stuff they want costs money. When your child know that the things they want cost money, they will become very motivated to save up for the object they so desperately want.

- Set an example. Little eyes are watching you so it's important that you are setting a good example for them to follow. Try not to argue with your partner about money in front of your child. It will only make them worried and get them to believe that arguing about money is a norm.

Tweens

- You already know that I do not believe in allowances for children, whether or not they are based on doing chores or getting good grades. An alternative is to give commissions. You shouldn't be rewarding your child for sitting on the couch all day or doing homework they have been assigned. Encourage and require them to work for their money. Have them sweep the kitchen floor, do the dishes, do the laundry, and more to help the family as a whole. When they work for their money, they can see just how hard they must work in order to be paid. This will also give them an idea of what it is like to have a real job.

- Show them that sometimes you have to prioritize your spending. If your child wants to buy new shoes, remind them that if they buy those shoes, they won't be able to buy that new dress or jacket they want. This will make them think about which item they would rather spend their money on and also the concept of "needs" versus "wants."

- Stress the importance of giving. Once they start making their own money, it might be a good idea to persuade them to choose a charity they would like to donate some of their money to. This simple action will be very humbling to them by allowing them to realize the importance of money and giving. I prefer Kiva, a site where you can make micro loans of as little as twenty-five dollars to entrepreneurs in underdeveloped countries.

Teens

- Give them the responsibility of a bank account. Allowing your teen to have the responsibility of having a higher amount of money in a bank account, will allow them to be more conscious with how they spend their money.
- Teach them the danger of credit cards. I discuss this briefly in Chapter Ten and it is worth revisiting here. Once your teen turns eighteen, credit card salesmen will be chasing after your child to sign up for a credit card. If you don't teach them about why going into debt is a dangerous place to be, they could quickly fall victim to credit cards.

Your child's age and level of maturity will determine how you go about teaching them about money. This type of concept won't be easy to teach, but there are numerous techniques to use to get the message across. If you aren't the person to teach your kids about money, somebody else will, and you may not want that.

Indoor Cheap and Fun Entertainment

Sometimes it isn't always feasible to do activities with your child outside, due to inclement weather, allergies, or illness. You may also be having money problems so sometimes doing fun activities can be even more difficult. Just the cost of gasoline to go somewhere may make it difficult to fit into your budget. The list below suggests some free and inexpensive indoor activities that you and your child can participate in regularly.

- Cook, bake, and prepare foods with your child. Kids love to have opportunities to do things with you and helping in the kitchen is a great option to consider when looking for some cheap activities to do. Making pie crusts, pizza, and biscuits can be some of the most fun things for kids to do, because they enjoy the feeling of the squeezing of dough through their fingers. Who doesn't?!

- Make roads for toy cars using colored tape on floors. This activity will keep your child busy by playing with their toy cars on the makeshift "road" you built for them. It will keep them busy for hours and is a very cheap entertainment idea that takes little time in making.

- Have fun with arts and crafts. For many kids, finger painting and coloring is a great activity to do to fill their time. It can obviously be messy so ensure that if painting, you put some old newspaper down on your table to prevent messes and any hassle.

- Transform an old box into a slide. If you have a set of stairs and a big enough box, simply take the box apart and lay it flat on the set of stairs. This will act as a fun slide for your child to slide down on and is a very cheap alternative to purchasing a playground. Be sure though, that if you do decide to make this type of a slide, you're careful that no one gets hurt. Ensure that there isn't anything your child can bump into on the way down or any other dangers that could be looming.

- Make some tie-dyed t-shirts. This activity can be cheap if you have any plain t-shirts that you aren't wearing right now. All that you may need to buy is the dye for the shirts. This activity is a fun (but a little messy!) thing to do with each other and is something that, once the shirt is dry, can be worn together.

- Make a fort. Drape some blankets and pillows over some chairs in the living room and make a fort. Then have a picnic lunch inside your fort.

Sometimes Mother Nature has different plans for us, so having some fun things to do indoors is a bonus. It's an even bigger bonus when the things you do inside are fun, cheap, and offer you the opportunity to bond with your loved ones. These activities can provide hours of creative entertainment for even the tightest of family budgets.

Inexpensive Things to Do with Friends

We all run into money issues in our lifetime. Sometimes it's especially hard because all you want to do is hang out with friends and spend the money you don't have right now. And, sometimes friends just don't seem to understand what it is that you're going through.

So if you are having trouble convincing your friends to do things on the cheap side, be upfront with them. Ensure that if you don't want them to pay for you that you are straightforward about this. Offer up some alternative solutions which are more cost effective for you. Listed below are some cheap things to do with your friends when money is an issue.

- Host a spa day. Give each other manicures. Do each other's hair. You can also try some face masks and exfoliate your skin. This activity is very inexpensive as long as you have nail polish and hair products.
- Binge watch shows on Netflix or Amazon Prime. There are thousands of different TV shows on Netflix. You can all decide on a TV series and watch as many episodes as time allows together. All you'll need for this is a device to watch on and maybe some popcorn.

- Go to the park. There's so many fun things that can be done at a park. You can have a picnic, play on the playground, or just watch the people as they all pass by with their busy lives. You can play sports together in the park like baseball or basketball, or throw a Frisbee or football around or fly a kite. You can play friendly games or be competitive. Check for parks that are doing concerts, for something fun to do on an evening out with your friends.
- Play board games. Dust off those boxes of Monopoly and Scrabble from your closet. You can all hang out and play these games in small or big groups. You might even consider competing against each other. I can remember hearing an interview with actress and producer Jodie Foster when her two sons were younger. She said their favorite thing to do was to stay home and play board games as a family. It's an excellent bonding opportunity.
- Dust off your bicycles out and go riding around the neighborhood. This provides you with a great chance at getting outside and getting some exercise together.
- Go to the beach or a public pool. Not all beaches and pools require you to pay to get in or for parking. So grab your bathing suits, the sunscreen, and the flip flops. You can simply go swimming, lie out and get a tan, or play in the sand and build sandcastles. Don't forget the sunscreen!
- Hike. Go on a walk through the woods, parks, and nearby towns. Ensure that you have the proper walking wear because if not, you'll be complaining not even halfway through the walk. Go online or to the library to get the information you need about local hiking and walking trails.

- Visit a fire house. Most fire stations will arrange tours for kids. This type of activity is an exciting thing for preschoolers and elementary school children alike, and even my teenage granddaughter enjoys meeting the cute young firefighters. This activity is free and provides your child or children with exposure to possible career choices they can explore in the future. Bake them some cookies to bring a smile to their faces!

- Make sunflowers. This activity may cost you a little bit of money, but it shouldn't be too much. First, you'll have to take a variety of different sized Styrofoam balls and slice them in half. Then, using tacky glue, cover the rounded side of the balls with sunflower seeds. Cut petals from yellow paper and glue them to the flat side of the Styrofoam ball. Finish the project up by covering the back side with a circle cut from the yellow paper. Once your project is completed, attach some ribbons to your flowers and tie them to a tree.

- Go to a local or minor league sporting event. Local minor league baseball games near your home are usually free and are fun events to attend with your family. Who knows, someday one these players may be called up to the "show", which is another name for the major leagues.

- Volunteer. Volunteer work is always free and is a great learning experience for you and your children. There is an abundance of ways to get your little ones involved in the community. For example, there are homeless shelters where you may help out. Many towns have gardening clubs that help to spruce up the community. Take your pick with volunteer work, because there is plenty that needs to be done.

- Plan a treasure hunt. The things the children are looking for can be something simple like a new toy car or even an old toy that they forgot about, but which they will have fun rediscovering. Write out some directions for your kids to follow to get to the treasure. There are even smart phone apps that make this a fun activity on a regular basis.

- Create a dress up box. Purchase old and cheap clothing from thrift stores and any clothing you don't wear anymore, and place in a special box for your children to dress up in. Your kids can host a fun fashion show outside for you and friends.

- Collect sticks, pebbles, rocks, seashells, and leaves from outdoors. Then, cut cardboard into the shape of a square or rectangle and cut out a display area. Have your children decorate the cardboard. Once it's dry, glue the treasures to the cardboard and display in your home.

- Play sports in your yard. It does not matter what type of a sport you play, but just getting outside and playing baseball, kickball, basketball, tag, and other outdoor games with your kids is a great activity to take part in because it's active and costs nothing to play.

It's important that our children have the opportunity to bond with us. You can provide your kids with that opportunity by doing simple outdoors activities that don't cost much money. If you're trying to save money, these types of activities are a great idea to take part in.

Staying Healthy as a Financial Strategy

It's important that we all lead healthy lifestyles. It all starts when we're young, so it's key that when you're a parent that you enunciate to your little ones the importance of a healthy life. And being sick can be extremely expensive, whether or not you have health insurance. Here is a list of ways to help your child to stay healthy in their lifetime.

- Ensure that your kids get enough sleep. Kids should be getting about ten hours of sleep per night, more or less depending on age – speak with your pediatrician about the appropriate amount of sleep your child should be getting. Make sure that the bedtime routine is always the same. Get pajamas on, brush teeth, read bedtime story, then go to sleep. Keeping this routine simple and the same each night will help your child get to sleep faster and easier.

- Make sure your child eats healthily every day. Don't let them eat too much, if any junk food. It will make them slow and puts them at risk of being overweight and at risk for a variety of serious health issues. Connected to this is ensuring that your child drinks plenty of water. You want to be sure you keep your child healthy to prevent too many visits to the doctor, so the best way to do this is by encouraging healthy eating and drinking.

- Promote good hygiene. Ensure that your child is brushing their teeth, taking showers, and putting on deodorant if they're reaching puberty. You should also be sure that when they cough or sneeze, they do it in the crook of their arm, not into their hands. This won't necessarily protect them from germs, but perhaps these habits will be seen by their peers which will then hopefully come back to protect your child later.

- Take them to the doctor's for their yearly check-ups. This will help protect them from any serious issues arising. If they do arise, hopefully anything can be caught early. Going for yearly check-ups will also show your child how important going to the doctor's is to staying healthy.

- Make sure your child gets plenty of exercise. Suggest a sport for them to start doing. The list of active sports your child can do is endless, ranging from baseball, to swimming, and lacrosse.

- Kids need to stay away from smokers and vapers. Everyone can fall victim to second-hand smoking. When anyone is around someone who smokes, you are allowing yourself the chance of respiratory problems.

- Ensure that if your child gets a cut, it's cleaned out properly. The proper cleaning of an injury can help prevent an infection.

- Sick children do not belong at school. This will only spread the sickness your child has to other kids. Also, when you're sick, it is best to relax and rest to get better faster. Sending your child to school while sick will only prolong their illness.

By taking these precautions and teaching your child to stay healthy, you are not only teaching them to lead a healthy lifestyle, but you are also saving money by avoiding medical costs. By keeping your child as healthy as possible, you can avoid the doctor's office as much as needed.

About the Author

Connie Ragen Green is an online marketing strategist, bestselling author, international speaker, and mentor to people on six continents. She is a former classroom teacher, real estate broker, and residential appraiser who left it all behind to start an online business during 2006.

This change of direction with career, lifestyle, and goals occurred as she came to realize that she wanted something more from her life than what she was currently experiencing. This was the beginning of a new life, where anything is possible and everything unfolds in a magical way.

After struggling during her first year of entrepreneurship, Connie finally embraced the struggles of writing and technology, leveled up her work ethic, and continues to exceed her own potential in her life and business.

Making her home in two cities, Santa Barbara, California at the beach and Santa Clarita, California in the desert, Connie is active with a number of charities, non-profits, and service organizations. These include Rotary, an international service organization; Zonta, a women's business organization with the Mission of advancing the status of women worldwide; the Benevolent and Protective Order of Elk; the Boys and Girls Clubs of America; and SEE International, an organization dedicated to restoring the vision of people in many underdeveloped countries.

Becoming an online entrepreneur changed Connie's life forever. Once she became versed in online marketing and observed first-hand how powerful the effect was for people all over the world, she began writing on a variety of topics, creating information products, speaking at live events and workshops, and mentoring people on how to build a successful and lucrative business they can run from home or from anywhere in the world.

Find out more and receive some relevant information right away by visiting https://ConnieRagenGreen.com and https://twitter.com/ConnieGreen to further connect with Connie and to begin your own journey of online entrepreneurship and thought leadership.

www.ingramcontent.com/pod-product-compliance
Lightning Source LLC
Chambersburg PA
CBHW060035210326
41520CB00009B/1132